BREAKING GROUND

BREAKING GROUND

Empowering Women in the Construction Industry

BY

BERNARD ARTHUR-AIDOO
Accra Technical University, Ghana

PRINCESS NAA KWARKAI QUARTEY
Accra Technical University, Ghana

PERRY RANSGREG NUNOO
Accra Technical University, Ghana

And

ALEX KWAKU ADZINKU
*Kwame Nkrumah University of Science and Technology
(KNUST), Ghana*

United Kingdom – North America – Japan – India
Malaysia – China

Emerald Publishing Limited
Emerald Publishing, Floor 5, Northspring, 21-23 Wellington Street, Leeds LS1 4DL

First edition 2024

British Library Cataloguing in Publication Data
A catalogue record for this book is available from the British Library

ISBN: 978-1-83549-639-8 (Print)
ISBN: 978-1-83549-638-1 (Online)
ISBN: 978-1-83549-640-4 (Epub)

INVESTOR IN PEOPLE

To the Building Technology Department, Accra Technical University.
For the unwavering love, encouragement and sacrifices that the department
members have made to support our dream. Your belief in us has guided us
through every chapter of our lives. This book is a tribute to your enduring
faith and the values you have instilled in us. Thank you for always believing in
us, even when we doubted ourselves.

CONTENTS

FOREWORD

It is with great pleasure that I introduce you to the pages of Ground Breaking: Empowering Women in the Construction Industry. As I had the privilege of perusing its contents before publication, we found ourselves drawn into a world of profound insight, captivating narratives and thought-provoking analyses. In this foreword, we aim to provide a glimpse into the richness that awaits you within these chapters. From the outset, it became evident that the authors have poured not only their intellect but also their heart and soul into this work. The result is a tapestry of ideas woven with precision and passion, inviting readers to embark on a journey of exploration and discovery.

Authors have a remarkable ability to distill complex concepts into accessible narratives, making even the most intricate subjects comprehensible to readers of all backgrounds. Whether you are a seasoned scholar or a curious novice, you will find *Ground Breaking: Empowering Women in the Construction Industry* to be both engaging and enlightening. Throughout these pages, authors tackle a diverse array of topics, ranging from women empowerment to gender equality and women in construction. Yet, amid this diversity, there exists a common thread, a commitment to fostering understanding, empathy and dialogue in an increasingly complex world.

What struck me most about *Ground Breaking: Empowering Women in the Construction Industry* is its relevance. In an era defined by rapid change and uncertainty, authors offer insights that are not only timely but also timeless. By grounding their analysis in both historical context and contemporary relevance, they shed light on pressing issues while also providing a framework for understanding their broader significance. It is my sincere hope that *Ground Breaking: Empowering Women in the Construction Industry* will find its way into the hands of readers around the world, enriching their lives and expanding their horizons in ways they never thought possible.

PREFACE

Welcome to the journey of *Ground Breaking: Empowering Women in the Construction Industry*. As you hold this book in your hands, you are about to embark on a voyage through ideas, knowledge and perspectives that I hope will resonate with you deeply.

This preface serves as a compass, guiding you through the intentions, inspirations and aspirations that have fuelled the creation of this book. Within these pages lie not just words but fragments of experiences, insights and emotions woven together to form a tapestry of understanding. Writing *Ground Breaking: Empowering Women in the Construction Industry* has been an odyssey – a labour of love and passion. It emerged from a desire to explore, to question and to share. Each chapter is a reflection of countless hours spent pondering, researching and crafting, with the hope of offering something meaningful to those who seek it.

Throughout this book, you will encounter diverse perspectives, challenging ideas and perhaps even moments of introspection. I aim to spark conversation and to invite you into a dialogue that extends beyond the confines of these pages. As you delve into the chapters ahead, I encourage you to approach them with an open mind and a curious heart. Engage with the content, question it, challenge it and allow it to challenge you in return. For it is through this exchange of ideas that we grow, learn and evolve.

I extend my deepest gratitude to those who have supported us on this journey, mentors, friends and loved ones who have offered encouragement, feedback and unwavering belief in the value of this endeavour. And to you, dear reader, thank you for joining me on this expedition. May *Ground Breaking: Empowering Women in the Construction Industry* serve as a guiding light, illuminating new paths of understanding and inspiring you to embark on your quest for knowledge and wisdom.

ACKNOWLEDGEMENTS

Writing a book is never a solitary endeavour; it is the culmination of support, encouragement and collaboration from numerous individuals. As we reflect on the journey of bringing *Ground Breaking: Empowering Women in the Construction Industry* to fruition, we are grateful for the many people who have contributed to its creation.

First and foremost, we would like to express our deepest appreciation to Mr Seth Allotey, whose unwavering support and belief in this project provided the foundation upon which it was built. Your guidance, encouragement and insightful feedback were invaluable every step of the way.

We are also grateful to Mr Mark Brookman-Amisah and Mr Gladstone Kportufe for their expertise and assistance. Your dedication to excellence and attention to detail greatly enhanced the quality of this book.

To our friends and family, thank you for your patience, understanding and words of encouragement during the writing process. Your unwavering support sustained us through the inevitable challenges and doubts, and we are profoundly grateful for your presence in our lives.

We would like to extend our appreciation to the team at Emerald, whose professionalism, enthusiasm and expertise have been instrumental in bringing this book to publication. Your commitment to excellence and passion for sharing knowledge has made this collaboration a truly rewarding experience.

Finally, to the readers of *Ground Breaking: Empowering Women in the Construction Industry*, thank you for your interest and engagement. It is our sincere hope that this book will inform, inspire and provoke thought and that it will spark meaningful conversations and reflections long after its pages have been turned.

1

CONSTRUCTION AND ITS WORKFORCE

ABSTRACT

Chapter one of this valuable book focuses primarily on the construction industry and emphasises on thematic areas such as industry entities, including its social and economic impact supported by the workforce within the industry. The workforce, which consists of a wide variety of training, semi-skilled and unskilled labourers, is crucial to the building sector. These people are vital to the conception, management and accomplishment of construction projects in various industries. The chapter also highlights the lack of female gender involvement and how the gender gap would be filled.

Keywords: Construction; female; labour; skill; unskill; workforce

1. INTRODUCTION

The book *Breaking Ground: Empowering Women in the Construction Industry* provides a thorough analysis of the obstacles, chances and programs meant to advance gender equality and empowerment in the historically male-dominated building sector. This groundbreaking study explores the many dimensions of the construction sector, illuminating the obstacles that women encounter and providing guidance on tactics for promoting equality and inclusivity. For an extended period, the construction industry has been marked by a gender disparity, wherein women constitute a minority within the workforce. The objective of this book is to investigate the reasons behind the underrepresentation of women in construction-related roles, with a focus on historical background, societal standards and organizational dynamics. 'Breaking Ground' offers a road map for removing obstacles and fostering an inclusive construction workplace by looking at the experiences of women who have successfully navigated this field and case studies of businesses enacting progressive practices. For those working in the construction business, legislators and advocates who want to make the industry a more equal and inclusive place for women, 'Breaking Ground' is an invaluable resource. With an emphasis on breaking down barriers, promoting inclusivity and opening doors for women, 'Empowering Women in the Construction Industry' offers an engaging look into the ever-changing world of the construction industry. This effort aims to break down barriers, dispel myths and advance an empowerment and equality-focused culture in a typically male-dominated field. Through an exploration of the distinct obstacles encountered by females in the construction industry and the presentation of triumphant tales, this project seeks to stimulate transformation and augment the continuous discourse around gender parity in professional settings. 'Empowering Women in the Construction Industry' is a blueprint for a more diverse and equitable future for the industry, not just a cry for change. This effort seeks to promote a culture shift that recognises the significant contributions made by women in creating the built environment through careful analysis and strategic ideas. This book encourages a change towards a future in which women are integrally involved in defining the built environment, thereby contributing to the ongoing discourse on diversity and empowerment.

2. CHARACTERISTICS OF THE CONSTRUCTION INDUSTRY

The construction sector is a dynamic and complicated one, distinguished from other industries by several unique features. Chapman and Ward (2003) opined that stakeholders, politicians and experts must comprehend these qualities to effectively navigate and leverage the potential presented by this complex industry. The construction sector typically uses a project-based business model (Construction Industry Institute, 2018). The scale, complexity and duration of projects can differ greatly; they might range from modest residential developments to massive infrastructural projects. This emphasis on projects adds to the industry's cyclical cycles and particular difficulties. Collaboration across a range of stakeholders, including suppliers, contractors, subcontractors, architects, engineers and regulatory agencies, is essential for construction projects to be successful. The achievement of the project is dependent on effective interaction and coordination due to the complex web of interactions within the sector. Construction projects frequently require large capital expenditures for labour, supplies and machinery. Due to its capital-intensive nature, the industry is prone to changes in interest rates, the state of the economy and the availability of funds (Chapman & Ward, 2003). The construction business must adhere to safety rules, building requirements and environmental norms. The regulatory environment is varied and region-specific, which makes project planning and implementation more difficult. The building sector depends significantly on both skilled and unskilled labour. There are craftsmen, engineers, project managers and labourers among the workforce's diverse members. The industry is characterised by Project budgets and schedules that are greatly impacted by labour productivity and availability. Inherent risks and uncertainties associated with weather, supply chain interruptions and unforeseen site circumstances are present in construction projects. For a project to be profitable and successful, effective risk management is essential (Chapman & Ward, 2003). The particular possibilities and challenges faced by stakeholders are defined by the features of the construction business, which include its collaborative environment, project-centric approach and responsiveness to technological improvements. In an ever-changing industry, this knowledge is the basis for wise choices and efficient administration. The construction industry is defined by its supply chain management, globalisation, diversity, fragmentation, cyclical nature and reliance on labour, regulations, technology, sustainability and project management. To negotiate the complexities skilfully of the industry and accomplish successful project outcomes, it is imperative that stakeholders in the construction sector, including contractors, subcontractors, suppliers, designers, project managers, policymakers and investors, have a thorough understanding of these characteristics (Construction Industry Institute, 2018). The construction sector can adjust to changing market conditions, tackle new issues and help create resilient, sustainable and inclusive built environments by embracing innovation, teamwork and sustainable practices.

3. ECONOMIC IMPACT OF THE CONSTRUCTION INDUSTRY

In both developed and developing nations, the construction sector is a major driver of employment, economic growth and infrastructural development. Its influence is felt in several sectors, impacting important economic metrics including GDP, employment and investment levels (Deloitte, 2018). An important factor in a country's economic growth is the construction sector, which stimulates investment, jobs and the development of infrastructure. Its influence goes beyond the construction of actual buildings; it affects other industries and also adds to the general vibrancy of the economy (Deloitte, 2018). Policymakers, investors, and other stakeholders who want to capitalize on the construction industry's potential for long-term expansion must comprehend its economic ramifications. The construction industry's status as a key employment is among its main economic contributions. A wide variety of skilled and unskilled individuals, such as architects, engineers, project managers, labourers and support staff, can find employment in this sector. The creation of jobs has a knock-on effect on associated industries, which supports a healthy labour market. Projects in the construction business require a large amount of capital, which means large expenditures on labour, supplies and machinery. Because the sector is capital-intensive, demand for complementary goods and services is stimulated in addition to driving economic activity within the sector, which promotes capital formation and economic growth (Bhattacharya & Wardhana, 2017). A common indicator of the state of the economy is the construction sector. Increased public and private investment in building projects can boost economic recovery during recessions by providing income, jobs and business environment confidence. Bhattacharya and Wardhana (2017) further suggested that the real estate market and the construction sector are intimately related, with the former influencing housing affordability, rental rates and property values. The growth of the residential, commercial, and industrial real estate sectors is facilitated by construction activity, which affects consumer spending and wealth development. Wide-ranging employment, investment and general economic well-being are all impacted by the building business. Policymakers and other stakeholders can create plans that maximise the industry's potential for long-term economic growth by acknowledging its many contributions. With companies, capital, and talent moving across international borders, the construction industry is becoming more globally integrated (Yiu & Tang, 2017). Increased efficiency and innovation in the construction industry are the results of globalisation's facilitation of the transfer of best practices, technology, and information. Research and development (R&D) spending stimulates innovation, boosts productivity and increases competitiveness in the construction sector (GCP, 2019). Innovations in technology, such as robotics, green building materials and building information modelling (BIM), have the power to transform the construction industry and produce favourable economic results.

3.1 Social Impact of the Construction Industry

The construction sector is a potent force that significantly affects people's quality of life on an individual and community level, and it does more than just create infrastructure and buildings as asserted by Akintoye et al. (2000). Beyond the tangible buildings, the social effects of construction can be seen in areas like cultural enrichment, community development and general societal well-being (Akintoye et al., 2000). To build resilient and sustainable communities, it is imperative to comprehend and capitalize on this influence. Communities are shaped in large part by construction projects, particularly those that are centred on urban development and regeneration. Community revitalisation is facilitated by mixed-use developments, affordable housing initiatives and infrastructure upgrades that create a sense of pride and belonging. Apart from the financial advantages, the construction sector is a noteworthy job creator, offering a wide range of roles to people with different abilities. This industry promotes professional development and skill development by acting as a training ground for apprenticeships and vocational education. Communities' well-being is directly impacted by the social infrastructure that is improved through the building of schools, hospitals and recreational areas. Social cohesiveness, general community resilience and health are enhanced by accessible and well-designed public areas (Akintoye et al., 2000). The cultural diversity of societies is enhanced by construction projects that prioritise the preservation and restoration of old structures. By preserving a link to the past, these initiatives also strengthen community identities and characters, encouraging a feeling of continuity and legacy (Baccarini, 2019). Beyond only building tangible structures, the construction sector shapes communities and affects societal well-being as a whole. Community members are included in the planning and decision-making stages of successful construction projects (Chapman & Ward, 2003). Through this involvement, initiatives are made sure to meet the objectives and goals of the community, which promotes social cohesiveness and a sense of ownership. By acknowledging and optimising these societal contributions, the building industry can function as a constructive agent for community advancement and cultural enhancement (Chapman & Ward, 2003).

The construction industry contributes significantly to inclusive development, meeting societal needs and reshaping social landscapes (Baccarini, 2019). The sector may maximise its positive social impact while minimising negative impacts by placing a high priority on social equity, sustainable practices and community engagement (Akintoye et al., 2000). To make sure that building projects help to create dynamic, resilient and socially inclusive societies, collaboration between stakeholders, governments and local people is crucial. The construction sector may remain a driving force behind sustainable growth and constructive social change if it remains dedicated to ethical behaviour and meaningful involvement.

3.2 Environmental Impact of the Construction Industry

Despite being vital to the advancement of society, the building sector has long been linked to serious environmental problems (Acosta et al., 2021). The activities associated with building lead to ecological degradation through resource exploitation and waste creation. However, the business is moving towards greener practices as a result of a growing awareness of environmental sustainability. This section of the book informs how the construction industry affects the environment and emphasises how crucial it is to use sustainable practices. Massive amounts of raw materials, such as metals, aggregates and wood, are needed for construction projects. These resources' extraction and processing increase energy use, habitat degradation and deforestation (Tam & Tam, 2006). By recycling and using materials efficiently, sustainable construction techniques seek to reduce the depletion of resources. Although the construction sector is essential to the growth of the world economy, its operations hurt the environment. From resource extraction to energy consumption and waste generation, construction activities contribute to various environmental issues (Tam & Tam, 2006).

The building sector is highly dependent on limited natural resources, including water, minerals and timber. Soil erosion, habitat damage, and biodiversity loss can result from unsustainable extraction methods (Van Der Heijden et al., 2002). Using recycled materials, sustainable sourcing methods and alternative materials is necessary to mitigate resource depletion. A significant portion of greenhouse gas emissions is caused by the construction industry, mostly by the usage of heavy gear and cement manufacture (Acosta et al., 2021). Reducing emissions requires investing in cleaner building equipment, enhancing construction logistics and using low-carbon cement substitutes. Large volumes of waste, such as demolition and construction debris, are produced by construction activities. Reduce the environmental impact of waste associated with construction by implementing waste reduction initiatives, encouraging recycling and material reuse and embracing the circular economy. The construction sector can play a constructive role in environmental conservation as it adopts sustainable methods. The industry can help create a built environment that is more resilient and sustainable by using resources responsibly, cutting waste and designing with eco-friendliness (Acosta et al., 2021). The construction industry's environmental effect highlights the pressing need for innovative, sustainable practices, and regulatory interventions to reduce environmental deterioration and enhance ecological resilience. The construction industry may reduce its ecological footprint and support international efforts towards environmental sustainability and climate resilience by using sustainable construction practices, championing environmental stewardship and embracing the ideas of the circular economy. To promote innovation, drive systemic change and build a built environment that strikes a balance between human needs and environmental preservation, stakeholders, industry actors, governments and civil society must work together (Tam & Tam, 2006). By committing to sustainable development, the construction sector can play a constructive role in environmental conservation and act as a catalyst for a more resilient and greener future.

4. CHALLENGES IN THE CONSTRUCTION INDUSTRY

The construction sector is the backbone of contemporary infrastructure, defining skylines and promoting economic expansion. Beneath its impressive accomplishments, however, are a plethora of formidable obstacles that put the industry's participants' resiliency and flexibility to the test (Dainty & Bagilhole, 2000). These obstacles, which range from labour shortages to complicated regulations, require creative thinking and teamwork to overcome. Although the construction sector is essential to economic expansion, it faces several obstacles that could prevent development and sustainability. Historically, the construction sector has been reluctant to accept new technologies quickly (Ofori, 1990). One of the challenges is incorporating cutting-edge construction technologies into conventional operations, such as Building Information Modelling (BIM), robotics and automation. Adopting technology can boost productivity, cut expenses and improve project results (Dainty & Bagilhole, 2000). For construction industry specialists, navigating a complicated web of rules and standards is a major task. Paying close attention to local building laws, environmental restrictions and safety standards is necessary for compliance. Simplifying rules and encouraging uniform procedures can lessen the load on the sector. The environment is significantly affected by the construction sector. The perpetual challenge lies in striking a balance between environmental sustainability and economic prosperity. To lessen these difficulties, green building techniques, eco-friendly material adoption and sustainable construction approaches are crucial (Ofori, 2019).

The construction industry supply chain may be disrupted by international occurrences like pandemics and geopolitical tensions, which could result in delays and higher expenses. To overcome these obstacles, supply chain managers must embrace digital technologies, diversify their supplier sources, and create robust supply chain plans. Keeping construction workers safe is a constant struggle (Cordero & Roig, 2014). Construction sites continue to be dangerous places despite improvements in safety laws and procedures. Ensuring safety problems are addressed through strict adherence to safety protocols, ongoing training programs and technological advancements for site safety. The lack of qualified workers in the construction sector is made worse by changing demographics and insufficient training initiatives. The scarcity may be addressed and a competent labour force for the future can be guaranteed by supporting apprenticeships, vocational education and workforce development initiatives. The construction sector faces a wide range of formidable obstacles, from environmental concerns and regulatory compliance difficulties to labour shortages and safety threats (Dainty & Bagilhole, 2000). Industry stakeholders must work together to address these issues, embrace technology-driven solutions proactively and demonstrate a dedication to sustainability and innovation. Through aggressively addressing these issues and adopting a continuous improvement mindset, the construction sector can surmount barriers, improve project results and clear the path for a future that is more robust and sustainable (Cordero & Roig, 2014).

5. WORKFORCE IN THE CONSTRUCTION INDUSTRY

The workforce in the construction business is essential to its success, but it faces a wide range of opportunities and problems in a constantly changing environment (Braverman, 1974). Particularly in important trades and professions, the construction industry is beset by a continuous skills deficit. To close these skills and competency gaps and guarantee a trained and competent workforce, a proactive strategy for workforce development is necessary, involving strong training programs, apprenticeships and collaborations with academic institutions (Construction Industry Institute (2019)). The ageing workforce makes succession planning and knowledge transfer difficult. Construction organisations must put in place efficient succession plans, mentorship programs and efforts to draw in and keep younger people to lessen the impact of retiring workers. With the introduction of digital technology, construction workers now need to be digitally literate and able to adjust to new tools like construction management software and Building Information Modelling (BIM).

Through focused training programs, employers may up-skill their workers and increase their competitiveness in the digital age. Diversity and inclusivity have always been difficult issues for the construction sector (Ogunlana & Promkuntong, 2006). Encouragement of a more diverse workforce – including women and underrepresented minorities – brings different viewpoints and creative ideas in addition to addressing social equality. Important steps in this area include industry-wide initiatives, mentorship programs and fostering an inclusive culture. The construction industry is being impacted by the gig economy and the growth of flexible work schedules. New job models are being investigated by both contractors and employees. By offering flexible work arrangements, embracing remote collaboration tools and reassessing conventional employment structures, the sector must adapt (Ogunlana & Promkuntong, 2006). Occupational health and safety are critical issues in the construction business, which is still a high-risk sector. Protecting the health and safety of construction workers requires ensuring a safe working environment through thorough safety training, frequent inspections and the use of cutting-edge safety technologies (Braverman, 1974).

6. LINKAGES IN THE CONSTRUCTION INDUSTRY

The construction industry operates within a complex web of interconnected relationships, where various stakeholders collaborate to bring projects from conception to completion. The dynamic connections between clients and contractors are fundamental to the building business. Effective project outcomes depend on efficient communication, precise project specifications and cooperative problem-solving (Finkel et al., 2018). The partnership between contractors and clients is essential to any building project. Successful projects must have open lines of communication, a shared understanding of the objectives and straightforward contractual arrangements. The ties that the construction industry has with the economy go beyond the confines of individual projects. The economic effects of construction activities were investigated in the current study, highlighting the relationship between the building industry and economic growth. Diverse professions, such as architects, engineers, project managers and environmental consultants, are frequently involved in construction projects (Ofori, 1990).

Multidisciplinary cooperation that works is essential to completing projects successfully. Clear, up-to-date information about the connections to the construction sector sheds light on the dynamics of interdisciplinary teamwork in building projects. The relationships between technology suppliers and construction organisations are becoming more and more important as the sector embraces digital transformation (Cordero & Roig, 2014). Subsequent investigations examine the obstacles and possibilities associated with incorporating technology into construction procedures, underscoring the necessity of cooperation between technology suppliers and industry participants. The GDP, employment, and other associated sectors are all impacted by the construction industry, which makes a substantial contribution to the overall economy. The industry's crucial contribution emphasises how important it is for promoting development and economic prosperity (Finkel et al., 2018). Both the public and private sectors' rapid infrastructure development has sparked building activity and increased demand for goods in several important industries, including cement, steel, paints and chemicals, glass, wood and machinery and earthmoving equipment (Ofori, 2019). One important industry with significant growth linkages both forward and backward is the building sector. It covers all commercial endeavours aimed at constructing, remodelling, repairing or expanding fixed assets, such as buildings, and engineering-related land improvements (Ofori, 2018). In addition, the construction sector creates a significant amount of jobs and stimulates the growth of other industries through backward and forward connections. Any nation's construction industry is a complicated one, with many different players and extensive connections to other industries.

Several researches conclude that there are close connections between the building industry and other areas of the national economy. According to earlier research, 'linkage' is a method for economic development. These researches highlighted the importance of 'unbalanced' growth within the economy's supporting sectors as opposed to a balanced development of all associated economic activity. Because of its numerous backward and forward connections with other economic sectors, the building industry has one of the strongest multiplier impacts (Cordero & Roig, 2014). This suggests that there is a close relationship between the construction industry and a wide range of economic activities, meaning that changes in one sector will inevitably have an impact on other sectors as well as the overall wealth of a nation. Therefore, the construction sector is seen as a vital and prominent contributor.

7. GROWTH FACTORS IN THE CONSTRUCTION INDUSTRY

Numerous growth variables impact the construction industry, which is a major force behind global economic development, and define its trajectory. The construction sector is mostly stimulated by economic expansion. The need for additional roads, bridges, airports and utilities is fuelled by growing urbanisation and industrialisation (Bubshait & Al-Jibouri, 2003). A mutually beneficial link is fostered between the construction industry and economic development through government initiatives and private investments in large-scale projects that boost construction activity. The building industry is still seeing tremendous expansion due in large part to rapid urbanisation. Residential, commercial and institutional structures are more important as people move into urban areas (Ofori, 2019). Construction activity has been steadily increasing as a result of mixed-use developments, urban rehabilitation projects and smart city initiatives (Bubshait & Al-Jibouri, 2003). Technological integration creates opportunities for eco-friendly and sustainable building techniques while also speeding up the construction process. The demand for housing is influenced by demographic factors, including population increase and shifting demographics. In response to these changes, the building sector builds cheap housing, senior care centres, and environmentally friendly housing alternatives, among other residential complexes. In the construction sector, environmental awareness is becoming a key growth component. Sustainable design, integration of renewable energy sources, and green building techniques are becoming more and more important. The use of environmentally friendly construction techniques is fuelled by stakeholder awareness, government legislation, and certification schemes like Leadership in Energy and Environmental Design.

In today's era, characterised by an increasingly interconnected world, the realm of construction has witnessed a profound transformation. The influence of globalisation has been a catalyst that has enabled construction companies not only to expand their operations but to flourish in a multitude of international markets. By embracing the concept of global interconnectedness, construction enterprises are breaking geographical barriers and capitalising on the shared ambitions and resources of countries around the world (Ofori, 2019). International collaboration plays a vital role in propelling the construction industry forward. Engaging in cross-border partnerships, firms can amalgamate different sets of expertise, share technological advancements, and combine resources for mutual benefits. This synergistic approach often results in more effective problem-solving and innovative strategies, paving the way for remarkable achievements in the construction field. The pooling of knowledge and resources from diverse backgrounds leads to a rich breeding ground for pioneering construction techniques and methodologies.

Investment without borders is another dimension that significantly contributes to the diversification and robustness of the construction sector. By securing foreign investments, construction companies can tap into a larger pool of funds, thereby increasing their capability to handle projects of various scales and complexities. This flow of capital not only underpins the financial stability of a company but also provides the necessary impetus for sustained growth and development across different market conditions (Bubshait & Al-Jibouri, 2003). Moreover, the construction sector has benefitted immensely from globally significant infrastructure projects that serve as beacons of operational and engineering prowess. These monumental projects are not just assets to the companies involved but often become iconic landmarks and linchpins for further economic activity. As a result, the successful completion of such projects usually propels companies into the international spotlight, enhancing their reputation and competitiveness on the world stage. For construction businesses that aspire to scale their activities internationally, navigating the financial landscape is of unparalleled importance. One of the primary growth enablers for any construction firm seeking expansion is access to adequate financial resources. This encompasses both cash flow and access to favourable financing terms. Due to the nature of the industry, large-scale construction projects mandate considerable capital investments that can only be met through effective financial strategies.

The construction industry's capability to initiate and manage sizeable projects intimately ties in with its ability to integrate with financial markets. Accessing private financing sources, such as venture capital, and investment banks and becoming attractive ventures for government funding methods significantly empower these companies. With robust financial backing, construction enterprises can undertake ambitious projects that may have been beyond reach otherwise. Favourable financial conditions amplify the capacity of construction firms to oversee grand endeavours (Ofori, 2019). Such financial support may include low-interest loans, grants, or other incentives that lower the entry barrier for initiating large projects. Access to a mix of public and private financing options ensures that construction entities are not solely reliant on one venue of funding which can mitigate potential risks and enable more aggressive growth strategies.

Additionally, the omnipresent need for capital from a range of sources, including financial markets, banks and individual investors, is a cornerstone for the proliferation of the construction sector. Without the assurance of sufficient capital, the ambitious visions of even the most innovative construction projects cannot transition from blueprints to reality. Hence, proactive financial planning and the cultivation of strong relationships with financial institutions are mission-critical for the ongoing expansion and viability of construction companies in the international market. In essence, while globalisation poses certain challenges for the construction industry, it also opens a plethora of opportunities.

Success in this arena is closely tied to the ability of companies to engage in international cooperation, secure cross-border investments, participate in globally vital projects and critically maintain access to flexible and substantial financial resources (Bubshait & Al-Jibouri, 2003). Those construction firms that adeptly navigate this dynamic environment clinch new arenas for growth and escalate their revenue potential exponentially.

The ability of construction companies to operate in a variety of markets has increased due to globalisation. International cooperation, cross-border investments and globally significant infrastructure projects all support the expansion of the construction sector. Businesses that rise to the challenges of operating internationally discover new opportunities for growth and income production. Growth enablers for the construction industry include access to cash and favourable financing terms. Large-scale construction projects frequently demand enormous investments, and the industry's capacity to carry out these kinds of endeavours is greatly impacted by its access to financial markets, private financing sources and government funding methods. Construction enterprises can embark on large-scale projects due to favourable financial conditions and enough access to finance. The availability of capital from financial markets, banks and individual investors is essential to the expansion of the sector.

The demand for construction services, infrastructure investment, and market potential are influenced by a range of economic, demographic, technological, regulatory and market factors, all of which contribute to the expansion of the construction industry. Stakeholders in the construction industry can identify strategic opportunities, capitalize on emerging trends and promote sustainable growth and innovation by comprehending key growth determinants and adjusting to changing market dynamics. To navigate market uncertainties, manage risks and position construction companies for long-term success in a dynamic and competitive global economy, collaboration, innovation and strategic planning are crucial. The construction industry has the potential to significantly contribute to economic development, improve quality of life and create resilient and sustainable built environments for future generations by prioritizing sustainability, resilience and continuous improvement.

8. BRIDGING THE GENDER GAP IN THE CONSTRUCTION INDUSTRY

Although historically dominated by men, the construction industry is beginning to recognise the need for more gender diversity. The key points of the gender gap in the construction industry are shown here, along with efforts and tactics that are meant to promote inclusivity and close this gap. Women have long been underrepresented in the construction sector in a variety of areas, from leadership positions to skilled trades. This has resulted in a considerable gender imbalance. Encouraging change begins with acknowledging this disparity. It is critical to promote and encourage women to pursue education and training in construction-related industries. Initiatives that support girls' education in Science, Technology, Engineering and Mathematics and offer financial aid to female students pursuing construction-related fields can contribute to closing the gender gap from the ground up. For a very long time, the construction business has been associated with heavy equipment, hard hats, and a workforce that is primarily male. In the construction industry, there is still a significant gender disparity despite advances in gender equality in other areas. In this field, women are still disproportionately underrepresented, and equal chances for female professionals are yet a ways off.

Although the construction business is known for being exciting and demanding, there is a noticeable gender disparity in it as well, with women being significantly underrepresented in a variety of roles. Analysing the underlying reasons for this discrepancy illuminates the intricate interactions between institutional, cultural, and societal elements that support gender inequality in the industry. One of the biggest obstacles facing women in the construction sector is still gender bias. Implicit bias in hiring and promotion procedures is frequently caused by stereotypes and previous beliefs about the talents of women. Consequently, this restricts the prospects accessible to females in the field. The underrepresentation of women in the construction industry at all levels is a serious problem. Not only are women underrepresented in leadership roles but also on building sites. It is imperative to confront and modify antiquated preconceptions and attitudes regarding the building sector. By highlighting accomplished women in the sector and providing good role models, the media and trade journals can change public perceptions and encourage more women to pursue careers in construction. It is critical to recognise and eliminate gender prejudice and discrimination in the workplace. A more inviting atmosphere for women can be achieved through training initiatives that increase awareness of unconscious prejudices and advance a culture of justice and equality. Creating networking and mentoring programs, especially for women in the construction industry can offer important support and direction. By bringing together seasoned professionals and recent graduates, mentoring programs promote professional growth and a feeling of community. Change-promoting organisations include trade associations, advocacy groups and government agencies. Building sector balance and equity are enhanced by cooperative efforts to address gender diversity, exchange best practices and support inclusive policies. A complex strategy, including educational programs, cultural changes and industry-wide collaboration, is needed to close the gender gap in the construction business. A diverse workforce may be fully utilised by the construction industry to drive innovation and long-term success by putting into practice policies that address structural issues and promote inclusivity.

The gender disparity in the construction sector is a complex problem with roots in societal standards, historical prejudices and structural impediments that support exclusion and inequality. A more inclusive, egalitarian and sustainable construction industry that maximises the potential of every employee, regardless of gender, can be achieved by stakeholders by identifying and resolving the underlying causes of this discrepancy. The industry can lead good change and innovation in the coming years by working together to promote diversity, dispel prejudices and create inclusive work environments. Systemic obstacles, cultural preconceptions and professional difficulties that prevent women from partici-pating in and advancing in construction careers are the main causes of the gender gap in the sector. All industry stakeholders – employers, legislators, academic institutions, trade associations and advocacy groups – must work together to address the gender gap. The building industry can foster a more welcoming and equitable workplace where women have equal chances to achieve and flourish by fostering diversity, equity and inclusion; putting supportive policies and pro-cedures into place; and confronting gender stereotypes. By utilising a wider range of expertise and viewpoints, closing the gender gap in the construction industry benefits not only women but also creativity, sustainability and competitiveness. The construction sector can lead the way in promoting gender equality via concerted effort and dedication.

BIBLIOGRAPHY

Acosta, R. I., Serrano, J. P., Serna, A. F., Botero, S., & Osorio, A. F. (2021). Environmental sustainability in construction: A systematic review. *Sustainability*, *13*(10), 5724.

Akintoye, A., & Fitzgerald, S. (2000). Analysis of factors influencing project cost estimating practice. *Construction Management & Economics*, *18*(1), 77–89.

Baccarini, D. (2019). The project definition rating index (PDRI) is a tool for construction project management. *International Journal of Project Management*, *37*(3), 463–478.

Bhattacharya, M., & Wardhana, N. A. (2017). The role of infrastructure investment in economic development: A global perspective. *Journal of Infrastructure, Policy, and Development, 1*(2), 150–176.

Braverman, H. (1974). *Labor and monopoly capital: The degradation of work in the twentieth century.* Monthly Review Press.

Bubshait, A. A., & Al-Jibouri, S. H. S. (2003). Effect of interest rate on the construction industry. *Journal of Construction Engineering and Management, 129*(4), 399–405.

Carmona, M., Heath, T., Oc, T., & Tiesdell, S. (2010). *Public places, urban spaces: The dimensions of urban design.* Routledge.

Catalyst. (2019). *Quick take: Women in construction.* https://www.mdpi.com/2073-4344/9

Chapman, C., & Ward, S. (2003). *Project risk management: Processes, techniques, and insights.* John Wiley & Sons.

CIOB. (2018). *Understanding construction workforce management in a changing global environment: A guide to improve productivity and labour relations.* https://www.ciob.org/media-centre/news/ciob-annual-report-2018

CIOB. (2019). *The role of the construction manager: A European survey.* https://www.ciob.org/media-centre/news/ciob-annual-report-2018

Construction Industry Institute. (2017). *Construction industry institute research team 314 – Workforce planning and development for the construction industry.* https://www.construction-institute.org/

Construction Industry Institute. (2018a). *Workforce development strategies for the construction industry.* https://www.construction-institute.org/

Construction Industry Institute. (2018b). *Women in construction: A study of company best practices.* https://www.constructioninstitute.org/scriptcontent/custom/ebook/Women_in_Construction_FINAL.pdf

Construction Industry Institute. (2019). *Workforce development strategies: Building the future of the construction industry.* https://www.construction-institute.org/

Construction Industry Training Board (CITB). (2018). *Increasing diversity and inclusion in construction.* https://www.citb.co.uk

Construction Industry Training Board (CITB). (2021). *Construction skills network report for the United Kingdom.* https://www.citb.co.uk

Cordero, R., & Roig, J. L. (2014). The construction sector in the European Union: Performance and economic importance. *Procedia Economics and Finance, 14*, 19–28.

Dainty, A., & Bagilhole, B. (2000). The marginalization of women in the construction industry. *Construction Management & Economics, 18*(2), 239–248.

Deloitte. (2018). *Global powers of construction 2018.* https://td.org

Eichholtz, P., Hartzell, D. J., & Hoesli, M. (2019). Economic risk factors and the returns on sustainable investment: Evidence from the European commercial real estate market. *Journal of Portfolio Management, 45*(1), 107–117.

European Commission. (2021). *Construction 2050: Building tomorrow's Europe today.*

European Institute for Gender Equality. (2021). *Gender equality in the construction sector.* https://eige.europa.eu

Finkel, E. J., Eastwick, P. W., & Reis, H. T. (2018). Replicability and other features of a high-quality science: Toward a balanced and empirical approach. *Journal of Personality and Social Psychology, 113*(2), 244–253.

Global Construction Perspectives (GCP). (2019). *Global construction outlook to 2030.* https://globalabc.org/sites/default/files/2020-03/GSR2019.pdf

Gyourko, J., & Molloy, R. (2015). *Regulation and housing supply.* National Bureau of Economic Research Working Paper No. 20536. https://doi.org/10.1016/B978-0-444-59531-7.00019-3

Hallowell, M., & Grilo, A. (2016). Breaking ground: Women in construction management. *Journal of Management in Engineering, 32*(1), 04015033.

Hillebrandt, P. M. (2017). *Economic theory and the construction industry.* Routledge.

Hopfe, C. J., Jones, K. G., Roelich, K. E., Owen, A., & Lomas, K. J. (2015). Embodied and operational environmental impacts: An input–output and structural path analysis of the UK building stock. *Building and Environment, 91*, 103–112.

International Energy Agency. (2019). *The future of construction: Opportunities and challenges for sustainable buildings.* https://www.iea.org/reports/world-energy-outlook-2019

ISO 14040. (2006). *Environmental management – Life cycle assessment – Principles and framework.* International Organization for Standardization.

Kanter, R. M. (1977). *Men and women of the corporation.* Basic Books.

Kibert, C. J. (2008). *Sustainable construction: Green building design and delivery.* John Wiley & Sons.

Li, H., Shen, L., & Cheung, M. C. M. (2020). BIM for sustainable building and construction. *Journal of Cleaner Production, 248.*

Lingard, H., & Rowlinson, S. (2005). *Occupational health and safety in construction project management.* Taylor & Francis.

Loosemore, M., & Raftery, J. (2006). The complexity of construction management. *Journal of Construction Engineering and Management, 132(6),* 561–568.

Love, P. D., Lingard, H., & Rowlinson, S. (2013). Modelling collaborative work in construction: Insights from empirical research. *Construction Management & Economics, 31(11),* 1137–1153.

Lu, W., Yuan, H., & Baumgartner, R. (2010). Sustainable construction waste management strategic model: Hong Kong study. *Journal of Construction Engineering and Management, 136(2),* 204–215.

Mavin, S., & Bryans, P. (2002). Gender, power and management discourse. *Women in Management Review, 17(7/8),* 348–360.

McKinsey & Company. (2017). *Reinventing construction through a productivity revolution.* https://www.mckinsey.com/capabilities/strategy-and-corporate-finance/our-insights/economic-conditions-snapshot-march-2017-mckinsey-global-survey-results

Miyamoto, A., Tezel, A., & Papadonikolaki, E. (2013). Productivity improvement of construction projects through lean design management. *Architectural Engineering and Design Management, 9(1),* 13–23.

National Association of Women in Construction (NAWIC). (2020a). *NAWIC workforce report.* https://www.nawic.org/nawic/Files/NAWICNews/2020/NAWICWorkforceReport2020.pdf

National Association of Women in Construction (NAWIC). (2020b). *Advancing women in construction: An NAWIC resource guide*. https://nawic.org

Ofori, G. (1990). Construction industry development: Issues and challenges. *Building Research & Information, 18*(2), 71–77.

Ofori, G. (2018). The impact of the construction industry on the economy of Singapore. *Journal of Construction Engineering and Management, 144*(4), 04018005.

Ofori, G. (2019). *Building delivery: Managing the building process and its products*. Routledge.

Ogunlana, S. O., & Promkuntong, K. (2006). Construction professionals' leadership styles and their impact on job satisfaction. *Engineering Construction and Architectural Management, 13*(3), 254–276.

Rowlinson, S. (2017). People in project management: A glimpse beyond our boundaries. *International Journal of Project Management, 35*(3), 546–556.

Sandberg, A. (2005). Natural construction and building biology. *Building and Environment, 40*(9), 1249–1263.

Shen, L., Yuan, H., & Shen, L. (2018). Assessment of environmental impact from construction projects. Through a life cycle perspective. *International Journal of Environmental Research and Public Health, 15*(7), 1524.

Simmons, J. L., & Dulebohn, J. H. (2005). High-performance work systems and organizational performance: Bridging theory and practice. In *Research in personnel and human resources management* (Vol. 24, pp. 53–101). Elsevier.

Smith, N. J., & Love, P. E. (2001). Towards a theory of construction as production. *Australian Journal of Information Systems, 9*(2), 96–109.

Talen, E. (2013). *City rules: How regulations affect urban form*. Island Press.

Tam, V. W. Y., & Tam, C. M. (2006). Environmental performance of construction waste: Comparing three eco-management tools. *Resources, Conservation and Recycling, 46*(4), 442–459.

Tezel, A., & Aziz, Z. (2017). BIM-based approach for evaluating energy performance of residential buildings in early design phase. *Journal of Construction Engineering and Management, 143*(12), 04017075.

Tezel, A., Lee, J. K., & Alshawi, A. (2015). BIM adoption and implementation for architectural practices. *Automation in Construction, 54*, 84–92.

The Boston Consulting Group. (2020). *How technology is revolutionizing the construction industry.* https://web-assets.bcg.com/40/84/ 80b567044409b74c32806275a3c1/bcg-2020-annual-sustainability- report-apr-2021-r2.pdf

Tiesdell, S., Oc, T., Heath, T., & Carmona, M. (2001). Urban design in the real estate development process: A case study of Bedford-Stuyvesant, Brooklyn, NY. *Journal of Urban Design, 6*(3), 257–281.

United Nations. (2015). *Transforming our world: The 2030 agenda for sustainable development.* https://sdgs.un.org/goals

United Nations. (2019). *World urbanization prospects 2018.* https://www. scirp.org/reference/referencespapers?referenceid=2907695

United Nations Environment Programme. (2017). *Global status report 2017: Towards a zero-emission, efficient, and resilient buildings and construction sector.*

U.S. Green Building Council. (2021). *LEED rating system.* https://worldgbc. org/article/annual-report-2022

Van Der Heijden, J., Duijnhoven, J., & van Buuren, A. (2002). Environmental impact assessment as learning process: Towards a sustainable future for the built environment. *Journal of Environmental Assessment Policy and Management, 4*(03), 259–285.

Wahlberg, T. (2009). *The three features that distinguish the construction industry with the manufacturing.* http://www.sagepub.com/ journalsProdDesc.nav?prodId=Journal200904

Winch, G. M. (2010). *Managing construction projects.* John Wiley & Sons.

Wirth, L. (2001). *Breaking through the glass ceiling: Women in management.* Wiley.

Women in Construction Operations (WiOPS). (2021). WiOPS – Women in Construction Operations. https://www.bigrentz.com/blog/women- construction

World Green Building Council. (2020). *Net zero carbon buildings: A framework definition.* https://worldgbc.org/wgbw2020

Yiu, C. Y., & Tang, E. C. (2017). The economic impact of construction activity in Hong Kong. *Habitat International, 60*, 52–58.

2

FEMALE GENDER IN CONSTRUCTION

ABSTRACT

This part of the book emphasises gender-related concerns in the construction industry as well as career knowledge from a gender perspective. The construction sector has always been seen as a field dominated by men due to its hard-working conditions, large equipment and ingrained gender conventions. However, as cultural perceptions change and diversity is valued more, women's contributions to the construction industry are becoming more widely acknowledged. By examining the difficulties women encounter, the chances for their empowerment and the revolutionary effects of gender diversity in the sector, this introduction seeks to shed light on the role of women in construction.

Keywords: Female; construction; cultural; diversity; empowerment; gender

1. INTRODUCTION

Throughout history, there has been a notable gender gap in the construction business, with women under-represented in several key roles. But in recent times, there has been a greater focus on advancing gender diversity and inclusivity, which has raised awareness of women's involvement in the construction industry. This change in emphasis has spurred significant conversations and actions meant to address the obstacles and chances encountered by women trying to make a name for themselves in the construction sector. Researchers and academics have been interested in the topic of gender inequality in the building business. The construction business has historically

been dominated by men, according to research, and women face many
obstacles to entry and progress. As a result, there isn't much gender diversity in
impacting organisational culture and performance. Women who have wanted
to work in construction have historically faced many obstacles and prejudices.
Because of stereotypes and established gender roles, there are few possibilities
for women to enter and succeed in the construction sector. These roles are
typically associated with the belief that particular roles are only suitable for
men. Further impeding women's complete integration into the construction
profession are problems including unequal compensation, a lack of mentorship and workplace discrimination. The important contributions that women
can make to the construction sector are becoming increasingly acknowledged,
despite these obstacles. Women contribute distinct viewpoints, abilities and
knowledge to the table, enhancing the industry with variety and creativity.
Furthermore, encouraging a gender-diverse workplace not only advances
social justice but also improves organisational effectiveness and the competitiveness of the sector as a whole. Women have been working hard to break
down barriers and make it easier for them to succeed in jobs related to construction in recent years. This has included putting focused recruitment techniques into practice, creating workplace regulations that are supportive and
promoting possibilities for education and training that are specifically geared
towards women who want to work in the construction industry. Advocacy
groups, industry associations and governmental authorities have been instrumental in promoting the interests of women in the construction sector and
advancing their rights to equitable treatment and opportunities. It is crucial to
assess the existing level of women's engagement in the construction industry
and pinpoint areas for development as the industry continues to adjust to
shifting societal norms and economic needs. By doing this, stakeholders may
cooperate to provide a setting that empowers women to lead, prosper and
make significant contributions to every aspect of the construction business.

2. GENDER IN CONSTRUCTION

Women have historically been disproportionately under-represented in a
variety of roles in the largely male-dominated construction industry.
Inequalities between men and women still exist in the construction industry
regarding job possibilities, pay and workplace culture. Nonetheless, there have
been initiatives in recent years to overcome these differences and advance
gender equality and diversity in the sector. This chapter explores the obstacles

that women in the construction industry confront, the advancements made in the area of gender inclusion and the room for growth.

In construction-related fields including engineering, architecture and skilled trades, women are still under-represented. In the construction sector, biases and stereotypes related to gender might provide obstacles for women looking for work and career growth. In the construction industry, harassment, discrimination and unfair treatment of women can occur, which can create a hostile work environment. It can be difficult for women in construction industries to juggle work in an industry that is dominated by males with family obligations. In the construction industry, women may face barriers to training, mentorship and job growth chances. Growing awareness of the value of gender diversity and inclusion in the construction sector has sparked conversations and actions to address gender inequality. Through networking events, mentoring programmes and lobbying activities, organisations, industry associations and advocacy groups are actively promoting gender equality and assisting women in the construction sector. Employers are putting methods in place to draw in and keep female talent, such as focused hiring campaigns, flexible work schedules and diversity education initiatives. Conventional gender conventions are being challenged and other women are being encouraged to pursue professions in construction by the rise of strong female role models and leaders in the field. Diversity quotas, equal pay requirements and anti-discrimination laws are just a few of the policies and efforts that governments and regulatory agencies are implementing to advance gender equality in the construction industry. Funding educational and training initiatives that equip young women with the skills and knowledge needed to pursue jobs in construction while also encouraging them to do so.

Enhancing the building industry's culture and mentality to promote better respect, inclusivity and assistance for women. To promote professional development and progress for women in construction, mentorship programmes and support networks should be expanded. Putting into practice and upholding laws that support work–life balance for all employees, encourage gender equality and stop harassment and discrimination. Encouraging industry stakeholders to work together and communicate, such as government agencies, advocacy groups, employers and workers, to address gender imbalance and bring about good change. The construction sector is moving in the right direction towards increased gender diversity and inclusion, even if there are still many obstacles to overcome. Through the implementation of focused tactics, raising awareness and advocacy and removing systemic hurdles, the industry may foster an atmosphere that is more equitable and inclusive, so enabling women to succeed. Reaching the maximum potential of gender diversity in construction will need sustained efforts and cooperation.

3. GENDER AND DEVELOPMENT THEORY

The realisation that development initiatives frequently failed to address the unique needs, roles and rights of women led to the formation of gender and development (GAD) theory. This theoretical framework supports tactics that advance social justice, women's empowerment and gender equality while highlighting the value of gender analysis in understanding development processes. An outline of gender and development theory, its main ideas and its application to development practice are given in this article. One of the fundamental concepts of gender and development theory is this. Understanding the historical and contemporary gender disparities that have shaped the construction sector requires this viewpoint. Women have historically faced many barriers to entry and professional progress in the construction industry, which has generally been dominated by men. The preconceptions, biases and gender stereotypes that society holds shape the organisational culture and labour mix of the construction industry. The gender division of labour is another issue that gender and development theory highlights and is especially pertinent to the construction sector. Throughout history, women have been under-represented in professions connected to building, partly because construction labour is thought to be more physically demanding and more suited for men. Due to this, women are under-represented in technical and leadership jobs within the sector and are concentrated in administrative and other areas. GAD highlights how gender roles, norms and power dynamics impact people's experiences and opportunities and how important it is to examine social, economic and political systems through a gender lens. According to GAD, patriarchy is a fundamental system of dominance and authority that gives men the upper hand and subjugates women in the home, workplace and public institutions, hence perpetuating gender inequality. According to GAD, women's empowerment is the process of giving them more agency, voice and access to opportunities, resources and decision-making authority on both an individual and group level. GAD recognises the intersections between gender and other social categories, including class, race, ethnicity, sexual orientation and age. These intersections give rise to multiple forms of privilege and oppression that influence people's identities and experiences. Participation and Inclusion: To guarantee that women's varied needs and viewpoints are taken into account, GAD promotes women's meaningful involvement and inclusion in all phases of development activities, from planning and implementation to monitoring and evaluation. Including gender analysis and concerns into all facets of development planning, policies, programmers and projects is achieved through the use of gender mainstreaming, which is encouraged by GAD. GAD places a strong emphasis on the promotion and defense of women's rights, which include freedom from discrimination and violence as well as the rights to work, education, health care and property ownership. Efforts to increase the leadership of women, decision-making and skill sets so they can contribute more effectively to development processes are called for by GAD. Institutional Change: GAD promotes institutional changes that upend patriarchal institutions and practices in governmental agencies, non-governmental organisations and other development groups to create settings that promote women's empowerment and gender equality. GAD acknowledges the significance of community-based projects, women's groups and grassroots movements in furthering these goals. A crucial framework for comprehending the intricate interactions between gender dynamics and development processes is provided by gender and development theory. Practitioners and policymakers can work towards more inclusive, equitable and sustainable development outcomes that prioritise women's rights, empowerment and well-being by incorporating gender analysis into development practice and policies.

4. GENDER GAP IN THE CONSTRUCTION INDUSTRY

The construction sector has historically been marked by a notable gender disparity, wherein women are comparatively under-represented in diverse roles and encounter multiple obstacles in their pursuit of equal opportunities and career progression. Gender differences continue to exist in the industry despite initiatives to increase diversity and inclusion. The causes, effects and possible solutions for promoting greater gender equality and representation are all examined in this chapter on the gender gap in the construction sector. In the construction business, women are mostly found in support, clerical and administrative professions, while men predominate in specialised trades and leadership roles. The idea that construction is a field dominated by men is fuelled by gender stereotypes and biases, which deters women from pursuing employment in construction-related fields. Workplace cultures in the construction industry may be characterised by discrimination, harassment and a lack of support for work–life balance, making them unwelcoming or

unfriendly to women. Women's representation and retention in the construction business are constrained by obstacles to training, apprenticeship
programmers and professional advancement chances. Pay disparities between
men and women in the construction industry are a common occurrence for
women, which exacerbates financial instability and inequality. Women's
earning potential and economic independence are restricted by the gender gap
in construction, which in turn exacerbates wider economic disparities.
Women's exclusion from the construction business robs the sector of a variety
of expertise and viewpoints, which may impede innovation and
problem-solving. The presence of women in top positions in the construction
sector leads to a dearth of varied viewpoints and opinions in the process of
making decisions. By putting diversity initiatives, outreach programmers and
focused recruitment tactics into place, construction companies can actively
recruit and retain women. Women can feel more supported and welcomed in
the workplace when inclusive policies and practices are established, such as
zero-tolerance rules for harassment and discrimination. Providing women-only
training courses, apprenticeships and mentorship programmers can help close
skill gaps and promote professional advancement. Campaigns to advance
gender parity, like laws pertaining to equal pay and anti-discrimination
guidelines, can assist in removing structural obstacles in the construction
sector.

More women pursuing employment in the construction business can be
encouraged by challenging gender preconceptions and biases through education, awareness initiatives and media representation. All parties involved in the
construction industry must work together to address the gender gap, including
employers, legislators, trade associations and advocacy organisations. In order
to develop a more varied and equitable workforce that benefits people as well
as the sector as a whole, the construction industry can adopt specific methods
to promote gender equality, cultivate inclusive workplace environments and
advocate for regulatory changes. Women are significantly under-represented in
the construction business, especially in technical, managerial and leadership
positions. This under-representation is a reflection of preconceived notions
about gender roles held by the general public, prejudices on the kinds of jobs
that would be best suited for men and women and work environments that
may be hostile or discriminatory to women. Because of this, women in the
construction sector frequently have obstacles to developing in their careers,
restricted access to chances for training and growth and difficulties locating
mentorship and networking assistance. The under-representation of women in
the construction industry, their restricted access to leadership positions and the

existence of a working culture that is predominantly male-oriented are just a few of the ways that the gender gap is apparent.

In efforts to increase the retention of women in construction consultancies, there was, nevertheless, minimal variation. The findings show that the most important strategies for keeping women in the workforce, according to both men and women, are more flexible work schedules, clear advancement standards, training programmes for returning to the workforce and outreach efforts to educational institutions. This supports the need for companies to implement creative strategic plans to alter the construction industry's patriarchal culture and move away from the archaic, traditional framework still in place.

5. GENDER INEQUALITY AND SUSTAINABILITY DEVELOPMENT

Gender inequality continues to be a widespread problem throughout the world, impacting many facets of society, including initiatives for sustainable development. In order to advance justice, resilience and prosperity for both the current and future generations, sustainable development seeks to address social, economic and environmental concerns. Nonetheless, because they exacerbate environmental degradation, restrict access to opportunities and resources and prolong poverty, gender gaps can make it more difficult to meet sustainable development goals (SDGs). The relationship between gender inequality and sustainable development is examined in this essay, which also identifies important obstacles and suggests tactics for promoting gender parity in the sustainability sector. Poverty, lack of access to healthcare and education and limited economic possibilities frequently disproportionately affect women, which can make it difficult for them to participate in initiatives for sustainable development. Furthermore, prejudice and violence against women might erect obstacles in the way of women's involvement in sustainable development decision-making processes. The advancement of gender equality, however, can benefit sustainable development. For instance, empowering women and girls via economic possibilities, education and healthcare access can result in better health outcomes, faster economic growth and higher levels of social and political engagement. Poverty disproportionately affects women and girls because of things like unequal access to financial resources, work opportunities and education. Achieving sustainable development and poverty reduction goals requires addressing gender differences in income and economic opportunity.

Gender disparities in healthcare and education can impede social and economic advancement and prolong poverty cycles. It is essential to guarantee that all genders have equal access to healthcare and education in order to develop human capital and promote sustainable development. Despite the important roles that women play in agriculture and food production, they frequently encounter obstacles when trying to get land, financing and agricultural resources. Encouraging sustainable agricultural practices and gender-equitable agricultural policies can improve food security and empower women farmers. Inequalities in gender can make climate change vulnerabilities and environmental degradation worse, especially for women living in marginalised communities. Incorporating gender viewpoints into environmental policies and plans for climate adaptation is crucial to foster resilience and accomplish objectives related to sustainable development. Due to their under-representation in political leadership roles and decision-making processes, women are less able to shape public policy agendas and solve gender inequality. Encouraging women to take on leadership and participate in politics is essential to fostering inclusive government and sustainable development. In order to guarantee that policies and programmers address the unique needs and interests of women and girls, gender issues must be incorporated into all phases of sustainable development planning, implementation, monitoring and evaluation. Putting money into programmers that support women's leadership opportunities, economic empowerment, access to healthcare and education will increase their resilience, agency and ability to contribute to sustainable development. Enhancing the gathering and evaluation of data on gender inequalities and how they interact with sustainable development metrics to provide evidence for evidence-based policy and programmatic changes. Men and boys must be included in the fight for gender equality as allies and change agents. Negative gender norms and behaviours must also be opposed, and positive masculinity must be promoted. Putting in place systems for tracking advancements towards the sustainable development objectives and gender equality, encouraging accountability and openness and allowing women and other marginalised groups to actively participate in decision-making. Achieving SDGs is significantly hampered by gender inequality, but it also gives a chance for revolutionary change. In order to create a more equitable, inclusive and sustainable future for all, policymakers, practitioners and stakeholders must acknowledge the connections between gender inequality and sustainable development and implement gender-responsive strategies. The achievement of SDGs can be significantly impacted by gender differences, which is why gender inequality and sustainability development are closely related. The term 'gender inequality' describes how people are treated differently and have different chances depending on their gender, whereas 'sustainable development' refers to addressing current demands without sacrificing the ability of future generations to address their own. Sustainable development may be negatively impacted by gender inequality in a number of ways. Poverty, lack of access to healthcare and education and limited economic possibilities frequently disproportionately affect women, which can make it difficult for them to participate in initiatives for sustainable development. Furthermore, prejudice and violence against women might erect obstacles in the way of women's involvement in sustainable development decision-making processes. The advancement of gender equality, however, can benefit sustainable development. For instance, empowering women and girls via economic possibilities, education and healthcare access can result in better health outcomes, faster economic growth and higher levels of social and political engagement. Encouraging gender equality can result in more inclusive and efficient decision-making procedures, which can guarantee that initiatives for sustainable development are sensitive to the interests and viewpoints of all people.

SDG 5 – Gender Inequalities, its aims and indicators are examined in-depth in this study. Moreover, to uncover patterns and correlations among the 14 SDG 5 indicators, explanatory data analysis, numerical association rule mining and Quant Miner are applied to the created Indian datasets on the aim. The associated pattern among these indicators is shown by the association rule mining that was done on them. While there is an 80% correlation between legal provision for women and women who have experienced physical violence, there is a perfect 100% link between the prevalence of crimes against women and legal provision for women.

6. CAREER KNOWLEDGE DEVELOPMENT

The field of career knowledge development comprises a diverse array of industries and experts committed to assisting people with their career exploration, skill enhancement and advancement in their careers. Rapid technology breakthroughs, changing labour markets and shifting worker demographics have all contributed to an increase in demand for professional knowledge development services. An overview of the career knowledge development sector is given in this chapter, together with an examination of major issues and trends as well as chances for innovation and expansion. In this field, experts offer individualised advice and assistance to people at different phases of their careers. They assist them in discovering their goals, interests and abilities as well as in navigating changes in their professions. Training providers give classes and programmers to build the transferable, soft and technical skills – such as problem-solving, leadership, communication and digital literacy – necessary for success in the job. Formal education and credentials are provided by educational institutions and certifying agencies to give people the skills and credentials needed for particular sectors and jobs. In order to assist well-informed decision-making and job search tactics, online platforms, career centres and libraries offer access to resources including job listings, resume templates, networking opportunities and career assessments. Professionals in particular disciplines or industries are connected through industry associations and networking groups, which offer chances for professional growth, mentoring and information exchange. Technology integration in career knowledge development services, such as digital credentialing systems, artificial intelligence (AI)–powered career exams, virtual career fairs and online learning platforms. The shift to an attitude of continuous learning, motivated by the necessity of constant up skilling and reskilling to adjust to evolving technological needs and employment requirements. The need for online resources for career advancement, virtual networking possibilities and skills training programmers that are suitable for remote work has surged due to the growth of telecommuting and remote work. Initiatives for career knowledge development should include more of a focus on diversity, equity and inclusion. This includes addressing systemic hurdles and facilitating opportunities for under-represented groups. Growing need for individualised professional development programmers powered by AI, machine learning and data analytics that are catered to each person's tastes, needs and objectives. Economic disparities and obstacles that prevent underprivileged and marginalised groups, in particular, from accessing high-quality career development services.

An inconsistency between the abilities that companies require and the skills that job seekers possess, underscoring the necessity of specialised training and alignment with industry demands. People must adapt and pick up new skills in order to be competitive in the workforce as a result of automation and rapid technology breakthroughs that are upending established employment positions. Challenges to recognising and transferring micro-credentials, non-traditional credentials and alternative learning and skill development methods. Agile solutions to new needs are required as a result of shifting labour market trends, employment patterns and workforce demographics that are influencing the demand for career knowledge development services. Extending and broadening the scope of online learning platforms to provide a variety of programmers, courses and materials that meet the needs of different learning styles, interests and professional objectives. To provide individualised advice, suggestions and assistance to people, AI-driven career evaluation tools, catboats and virtual career coaches are being developed. Developing and providing industry-recognised, skill-based credentials and micro-credentials in line with new fields and changing work requirements in partnership with industry partners. Designing and implementing specialised training programmes, staff development initiatives and talent management strategies in collaboration with businesses to address particular skill gaps and business demands. Creating professional knowledge development services that are inclusive, accessible and reasonably priced while taking into account the needs of a variety of groups, such as workers who are displaced, refugees and people with impairments. To help people navigate their career paths, learn new skills and realise their professional goals, the career knowledge development sector is essential. To fulfil the changing requirements of the workforce and support sustainable economic and social development, the sector must embrace technological innovation, address issues of equity and access and seize chances for growth and collaboration. The process of gaining knowledge and abilities relevant to a specific career or profession is referred to as career knowledge development. Career knowledge development is crucial for advancing careers and resolving gender gaps in the construction sector. It is well-recognised that obstacles to career advancement, such as restricted access to chances for training and development, frequently face women working in the construction business. By giving women the abilities and information required to progress in their careers, career knowledge development programmers can assist in removing these obstacles. It was shown that career development initiatives emphasising management and leadership abilities helped women in the construction sector improve in their careers. Likewise, it was discovered that mentorship programmes offering career counselling and assistance were effective in promoting career advancement for women in construction.

This contentious situation is interpreted in terms of the seemingly incompatible conceptualisations of knowledge. The organisation views knowledge as a resource that it wants to claim using procedures meant to provide flexibility in employment. This process, we argue, is not one-way; rather, the person builds up their expertise as 'career capital' in response to the uncertainties of reconstituted careers and employs employability strategies. By utilising Foucault's genealogical method, we contend that the aforementioned competition is a social phenomenon originating from the knowledge-power dialectic, which illuminates people's attempts to break free from the consequences of normalisation. It also represents the dynamic employment relationship and economic instability.

7. ATTITUDE OF GENDER IN THE CONSTRUCTION INDUSTRY

Gender preconceptions and biases have historically influenced perceptions regarding women's participation in the construction business, which has historically been controlled by men. These beliefs may affect women's access to career progression, retention and recruitment in the construction sector, which may exacerbate gender inequities in the field. Promoting inclusiveness, diversity and equality in the construction sector requires an understanding of and attention to gender attitudes. This essay examines the prevalent views on gender in the construction sector, points out obstacles and talks about ways to encourage constructive change. The idea that women are not fit for jobs in construction is reinforced by gender stereotypes that portray the sector as physically taxing and male-dominated. Initiatives promoting gender diversity may encounter opposition from the construction industry due to deeply ingrained cultural norms and practices that perpetuate gender prejudices. Workplace Atmosphere: Women may find it difficult to participate in and progress in the construction sector due to the macho attitude and locker room vibe. Due to prevailing gender prejudices, women in leadership positions within the construction sector may encounter opposition and scepticism, with questions raised about their qualifications and competence. Insufficient prospects for career progression and professional growth could deter women from pursuing enduring careers in construction, hence impacting retention rates. Adverse perceptions of women in the construction sector may discourage capable individuals from pursuing careers in the field and escalate the attrition rates experienced by female staff members. Toxic workplaces might have low morale, low productivity and dissatisfied employees due to hostile or discriminatory attitudes towards gender. Gender biases have the potential to cause qualified female candidates for skilled professions to be overlooked, which would exacerbate the talent deficit in the construction industry. Gender discrimination in attitudes and actions can put construction companies in danger of legal trouble and harm to their reputation, which can be detrimental to their ability to stay in business. Women's exclusion from the construction business restricts creativity and variety of thought, making it more difficult for the sector to adjust to shifting consumer needs. By educating and training industry stakeholders on gender diversity and inclusion, we may dispel preconceptions and raise understanding of the advantages of gender equality. Organisational change is largely dependent on the leadership's commitment to promoting inclusive workplace environments and carrying out diversity programmes. Creating networks of support and mentorship programmes for women working in construction can offer invaluable advice, connections and assistance with professional advancement. Employing collaborations with educational institutions and apprenticeship programmers, among other targeted recruitment and outreach initiatives, to draw and keep women in the construction industry.

Advocating, with the backing of government agencies and industry associations, for laws and policies that combat discrimination and advance gender equality in the building sector. Employers, workers, trade groups, legislators and other stakeholders must work together to address gender attitudes in the construction sector. Construction companies can develop a more diverse, egalitarian and long-lasting workforce by dispelling myths, promoting inclusive workplace cultures and putting specific recruitment and retention initiatives into place. The construction industry's negative views towards women must be addressed through a multifaceted strategy that incorporates training, education and cultural transformation. It was found that providing gender awareness training to construction workers raised their knowledge of biases and preconceptions based on gender as well as their support for efforts promoting gender equality. Informal learning and knowledge-sharing networks can also be used to develop positive attitudes towards women in the construction sector, in addition to formal training programmers.

8. MALE-DOMINATED TRAINING COURSES

The male-dominated culture of the construction industry, where specific trades and skill sets are traditionally associated with men, is often reflected in and reinforced by training programmers. Women who want to participate and excel in the construction industry may encounter obstacles as a result of the gender gap in training programmers. In order to advance gender diversity and equality in the construction sector, it is imperative to comprehend the difficulties posed by male-dominated training programmers and put inclusionary initiatives into practice. This chapter looks at the frequency of training programmers that are predominately male, looks at the obstacles that these programmers present for women and talks about ways to promote inclusiveness. Some skilled trades, like welding, plumbing, electrical work and carpentry, have historically been dominated by men, and female presence in training programmers may be lacking. Training programmers for operating heavy machinery, such as excavators, cranes and bulldozers, are primarily attended by men and are frequently seen as physically taxing. Although there may not be a gender bias in construction management roles, female enrollment in training courses and educational programmers may be lower than that of males in this profession. Construction workers must complete occupational health and safety training programmers, such as Occupational Safety and Health Administration (OSHA) certification; however, these programmers could not fully address gender-specific safety issues. Women may be discouraged from enrolling in training programmers in fields where males predominate due to stereotypes regarding the suitability of particular trades or occupations for men versus women. Female participants may experience feelings of loneliness, lack of support and restricted networking opportunities as a result of the under-representation of women in training programmers.

Training programmers with a preponderance of men may cultivate a hostile or unwelcoming atmosphere towards women, marked by discrimination, harassment and microaggressions. Training programmers may unintentionally perpetuate gender stereotypes or fail to take into account the special needs and experiences of female students, thus marginalising women in the construction sector. The lack of female mentors, teachers and role models in training programmers with a preponderance of male students can impede the career growth and promotion of women in the construction industry. Establishing focused outreach and recruitment initiatives, such as collaborations with educational institutions, neighbourhood associations and women's organisations, to draw more women to training programmers that are predominately attended by men. Creating welcoming and encouraging learning environments that value fairness, diversity and respect while addressing problems like harassment and discrimination. To promote women's professional growth and success in the construction sector, mentorship programmers, networking opportunities and access to female role models and industry leaders are offered. Training programmers should be reviewed and updated to make sure they are inclusive, gender-sensitive and take into account the needs and experiences of all participants, regardless of gender. Giving priority to inclusive practices and policies and empowering employers, training providers and leaders in the industry to promote gender equality and diversity in the construction sector. Women who want to participate and excel in the construction sector face obstacles due to training programmers who are predominantly male. More gender diversity and equality in training programmers and the workforce can be promoted by the construction industry by tackling gender stereotypes, creating inclusive settings and putting targeted recruitment, support and curriculum development methods into practice. These programmers frequently contribute to gender inequality by erecting obstacles in the way of women's advancement in the construction sector. Studies have indicated that training programmers with a preponderance of male participants can perpetuate gender norms and establish an atmosphere that is inhospitable to females. In addition, a lack of gender diversity in training programmers might reinforce biases and traditional gender norms, which will ultimately impede the advancement of women in the construction industry. The absence of role models and representation is another factor. Women may be less inclined to pursue certain careers if they don't see other women in them thriving. The under-representation of women in some training courses may also be attributed to a lack of resources and enabling surroundings. There is a gender gap that is being addressed. Institutions and organisations are putting policies into place to support and encourage women in industries where men predominate. These initiatives, which seek to dismantle obstacles and advance gender equality, include awareness campaigns, mentorship programmes and scholarship awards.

9. RECRUITMENT PRACTICES

In order to find, draw in and choose the best people to fill industry labour needs, recruitment procedures are essential. In addition to guaranteeing the hiring of outstanding personnel, successful recruitment tactics also support inclusion, equity and diversity in the workplace. This chapter addresses the significance of inclusive hiring procedures, looks at techniques for improving diversity in recruiting and investigates important recruitment practices utilised by a variety of businesses. Leveraging a variety of platforms to promote job opportunities and draw applications, including social media, corporate websites, professional networks and online job boards.

Employing proactive methods such as industry conferences, networking events, referrals and talent databases to find untapped potential and broaden the pool of prospects. Using applicant tracking systems software to handle candidate applications, monitor applicant progress and analyse recruiting metrics will help to optimise the hiring process. Assessing individuals' qualifications, abilities and organisational fit through initial screenings, interviews, evaluations and reference checks. Facilitating new hires' integration into the company and ensuring a seamless transfer into their roles by offering them complete onboarding programmers and assistance. Training hiring managers and recruiters about unconscious biases and how to lessen their effects on the recruiting process so that all candidates are treated fairly and equally. Looking for and actively interacting with candidates from a variety of backgrounds, especially marginalised groups including women, racial and ethnic minorities, LGBTQ+ persons and those with disabilities. To draw in a wide pool of applicants, inclusive job descriptions should emphasise diversity and inclusion values, use gender-neutral language and concentrate on necessary skills and qualifications. Partnering with schools of higher learning, community organisations and diversity-focused businesses to broaden recruitment networks, gain access to a variety of talent pools and advance inclusive hiring procedures. Monitoring and evaluating diversity and inclusion-related recruiting metrics, such as applicant demographics hiring rates and retention rates, to monitor progress and identify areas for improvement. Diverse teams enable organisations to be more creative, innovative and capable of addressing problems by bringing together a variety of viewpoints, experiences and ideas. Higher levels of engagement, satisfaction and retention are more common in inclusive workplaces where workers feel appreciated, respected and represented. Teams with a diverse membership tend to have stronger decision-making processes because different perspectives and ideas lead to more thorough assessments and superior results. Businesses that put a high priority on diversity and inclusion in their hiring procedures attract top talent looking for inclusive work environments and improve their standing as inclusive employers. Using inclusive recruiting procedures assists companies in abiding by anti-discrimination legislation, reducing legal risks and avoiding reputational harm brought on by discriminatory employment practices. Effective recruitment procedures are crucial for drawing in and choosing the best candidates to propel an organisation's growth. Organisations may create more creative, dynamic and productive teams that represent the range of skills and viewpoints in the work-force by putting initiatives to improve diversity and inclusion in recruitment into practice. Informal recruitment procedures, ads and brochures with pictures reflecting masculine values and interests, unstructured interviews, biased selection criteria and sexist attitudes are often the reasons why women are discouraged from applying for employment in the construction business. Many businesses still believe that women are unfit for certain jobs that have historically been held by males. Workers in manual trades, for instance, must have a respectable level of strength and fitness. Certain tasks, such as lifting and heavy operations, call for above-average upper body strength.

10. WOMEN IN THE CONSTRUCTION INDUSTRY

Although males have historically held the majority of positions in the construction business, in recent years, there has been a rising recognition of the valuable contributions that women can bring to the field. Women are increasingly choosing jobs in construction, adding a variety of talents, view-points and leadership attributes to the field despite confronting many obstacles. The experiences of women in the construction sector are examined in this chapter, along with the obstacles they encounter and methods for advancing gender diversity and inclusion. Long-standing misconceptions portray construction as a physically hard, male-dominated industry, which feeds prejudice against women and the idea that they are incapable of doing particular jobs. The culture of the construction industry, which is marked by macho attitudes, locker room humour and a lack of diversity, can make workplaces hostile to women and subject them to harassment, discrimination and isolation. Due to obstacles to recruitment, retention and progression, women are still under-represented in construction-related professions, such as skilled trades, engineering, architecture and leadership roles. It can be difficult for women to juggle the demands of a construction job with family obligations, especially in positions that call for long hours, travel and strenuous physical labour. When it comes to professional development tools, mentorship opportunities and support networks, women in the construction sector may not have as much access as their male counterparts. More women are entering the construction industry and seeking jobs in skilled trades, engineering and management roles as a result of initiatives to promote gender diversity and inclusion in the sector. Women are defying gender stereotypes and pursuing professions in construction as a result of the rise of strong female leaders and role models in the field. Through mentorship programmes, networking events and lobbying activities, organisations, industry associations and advocacy groups are actively promoting gender equality and assisting women in the construction sector. Policies and initiatives, including diversity quotas, equal pay requirements and anti-discrimination laws, are being introduced by governments and regulatory agencies to advance gender equality in the construction industry. Improving the presence of women in the construction sector requires funding training and educational initiatives that inspire young women to seek jobs in the field and arm them with the requisite knowledge and abilities. Although there has been progress for women in the construction sector, there are still obstacles to overcome before complete gender equality and inclusion can be achieved. The industry can foster a more fair and inclusive atmosphere where women may flourish and make valuable contributions to the industry's success by tackling systemic barriers, raising awareness advocating for change and putting focused ideas into practice. As initiatives to advance gender diversity and inclusivity in the sector have gained traction, there has been an increasing amount of interest in the engagement of women in the construction business. Women are becoming more and more prevalent in the construction industry these days, especially in positions like project management, architecture, engineering and sustainability. One research, for instance, focused on how more and more women are pursuing these careers and adding to the industry's diverse talent pool. The difficulties encountered by women in the construction sector are widely known, and these include problems with access to opportunities, professional advancement and workplace culture. Research has illuminated the obstacles faced by women in the construction industry, such as gender stereotypes, insufficient mentorship opportunities and difficulties juggling work and personal obligations. Several efforts have been launched to assist and empower women in the construction industry, such as networking events, mentorship programmes and policy advocacy for gender equality. Furthermore, organisations and industry stakeholders have taken steps to establish more welcoming and encouraging settings for women in construction as they have come to understand the importance of supporting gender diversity.

BIBLIOGRAPHY

American Society for Training and Development (ASTD). (2019). *ASTD handbook: The definitive reference for training & development* (2nd ed.). https://alastore.ala.org/content/astd-american-society-training-development

Arditi, D., & Balci, G. (2009). Managerial competencies of male and female construction managers. *Journal of Construction Engineering and Management*, *135*(11), 1275–1278.

Association for Talent Development (ATD). (2020). *Foundations of learning and instructional design technology*. https://td.org

Bersin by Deloitte. (2018). *High-impact talent acquisition: Key findings and maturity model*. https://www2deloitte.com

Catalyst. (2020). *Women in male-dominated industries and occupations: Quick take*. https://indigenouscleanenergy.com/our-programs/20-20-catalysts

Cockburn, T. (2018). Gender and the construction of training courses. *Construction Management & Economics*, *36*(1), 45–57.

Construction Industry Institute (CII). (2018). *Best practices for gender diversity and inclusion in the construction industry*. https://www.construction-institute.org

Construction Industry Institute (CII). (2019). *Advancing women in the construction industry: A guidebook to strategies and resources for success*. https://www.construction-institute.org

Cornwall, A., & Edwards, J. (2010). *Feminisms in development: Contradictions, contestations and challenges*. Zed Books.

Datta, N. (2019). Women in construction: A literature review on the role of women in the construction industry. *International Journal of Scientific & Technology Research, 8*(11), 231–235.

Diversity Best Practices. (2021). *Recruiting best practices*. https://www.societyfordiversity.org/workplace-diversity-inclusion-trends-for-2021

European Institute for Gender Equality. (2019). *Gender equality in the construction sector in the European union*. https://eige.europa.eu/publications/gender-equality-construction-sector-european-union

European Institute for Gender Equality (EIGE). (2019). *Gender equality in the construction sector*. https://eige.europa.eu

European Institute for Gender Equality (EIGE). (2020). *Gender equality in the construction sector: An overview*. https://eige.europa.eu

Haltom, S. (2018). *Bridging the gender gap: Strategies for attracting, retaining and advancing women in the construction industry*. McGraw Hill.

Harvard Business Review (HBR). (2016). *Why diversity programs fail*. https://store.hbr.org/product/harvard-business-review-may-2016/BR1605

International Institute for Sustainable Development. (2021). *Sustainable Development*. International Institute for Sustainable Development. https://www.iisd.org

International Labor Organization (ILO). (2020). *Skills for a resilient youth: Guidance for education and employability*. https://webapps.ilo.org/wcmsp5/groups/public/—dgreports/—dcomm/—publ/documents/publication/wcms_756877.pdf

Kabeer, N. (2005). Gender equality and women's empowerment: A critical analysis of the third millennium development goal. *Gender and Development, 13*(1), 13–24.

Lingard, H., & Francis, V. (2005). The construction industry and the gendering of professional practice. *Construction Management & Economics, 23*(3), 285–294.

Moser, C. O. N. (1993). *Gender planning and development: Theory, practice and training.* Routledge.

National Career Development Association (NCDA). (2021). *Career development facilitator training manual* (3rd ed.). https://www.ncda.org

National Association of Women in Construction (NAWIC). (2021a). *Women in construction: Building a diverse workforce for the future.* https://nawic.org

National Association of Women in Construction (NAWIC). (2021b). *Advancing women in construction.* https://nawic.org

Razavi, S. (2003). Introduction: Gender justice, development, and rights. In S. Razavi & S. Miller (Eds.), *From WID to GAD: Conceptual shifts in the women and development discourse* (pp. 1–22). United Nations Research Institute for Social Development.

Sen, G., & Grown, C. (1987). *Development, crises, and alternative visions: Third world women's perspectives.* Monthly Review Press.

Society for Human Resource Management (SHRM). (2021). *Effective recruiting strategies and practices.* https://www.shrm.org

Talent Board. (2020). *Candidate experience research report.* https://www.thetalentboard.org/cande-awards/the-cande-winners-latam-2020

Tilley, P., & Culshaw, M. (2018). Gender and recruitment in the construction industry. *Construction Management & Economics, 36*(5), 285–297.

United Nations. (2015). *Transforming our world: The 2030 agenda for sustainable development.* United Nations.

United Nations Development Programme (UNDP). (2019). *Gender equality and sustainable development goals.* https://annualreport.undp.org/2019

United Nations Development Programme. (2020). *Human development report 2020: The next frontier: Human development and the anthropocene.* United Nations Development Programme. hptts//hdr.undp.org

United Nations Entity for Gender Equality and the Empowerment of Women (UN Women). (2017). *Progress of the world's women 2017–2018: Transforming economies, realizing rights.* https://sdgs.un.org/un-system-sdg-implementation/united-nations-entity-gender-equality-and-empowerment-women-un-women

United Nations Environment Programme (UNEP). (2020). *Gender and environment: Gender equality for environment sustainability.* https://sdgs.un.org/un-system-sdg-implementation/united-nations-environment-programme-unep-44155

United Nations Women. (2018). Turning promises into action: Gender equality in the 2030. Agenda for sustainable development.

U.S. Bureau of Labor Statistics. (2021). *Women in the labor force: A datebook.* https://www.bls.gov/opub/reports/womens-databook/2021/home.htm

Wodon, Q., & de la Brière, B. (Eds.). (2007). *Gender and development: Evidence from the World Bank's 2007 gender action plan.* World Bank Publications.

World Bank. (2020). *Gender equality, poverty reduction, and inclusive growth.* https://elibrary.worldbank.org/doi/abs/10.1596/978-1-4648-1619-2

World Economic Forum (WEF). (2021). *The future of jobs report 2020.* https://www.weforum.org/organizations/holtzbrinck-publishing-group

3

WOMEN EMPOWERMENT AND EQUALITY

ABSTRACT

Gender equality and women's empowerment are essential for social progress and sustainable development. Gender equality and women's empowerment initiatives have gained traction in the formerly male-dominated construction sector in recent years. The purpose of this part of the book is to discuss the difficulties that women in the construction industry experience, the value of women's empowerment and the methods that may be used to achieve gender equality in the field.

Keywords: Construction; equality; empowerment; gender; male; women

1. INTRODUCTION

Building a just and inclusive society requires addressing gender equality and women's empowerment. Societies worldwide are realising how important it is to provide women equal access to resources, rights and opportunities. This chapter examines the many facets of women's equality and empowerment, examining historical background, current issues and the need for social change. The construction industry has traditionally been male-dominated, but women have made great strides in entering and advancing in recent decades. However, significant gender disparities persist. This chapter examines the importance of empowering women and promoting gender equality within the construction sector. The process of giving women in society equal rights, opportunities and resources is referred to as women empowerment. It seeks to provide women with the tools they need to reach their full potential and take meaningful roles in decision-making and advance social, economic, cultural and political advancement. Conversely, equality promotes justice and fairness by giving all people the same opportunity and respect, regardless of gender. Economic, social and political empowerment are all included in the notion of women's equality and empowerment. It entails confronting stereotypes, violence against women and discrimination based on gender. The goal of women's equality and empowerment is to establish a fair, impartial and inclusive society in which women are empowered to direct their own lives and make decisions on their own. The well-being of society and sustainable development depends on the empowerment and equality of women. Women may make major contributions to economic expansion, the fight against poverty and general social advancement when they are given more authority. It benefits women individually as well as their families, communities and whole countries. Women's empowerment and equality are pressing issues that have gained immense attention and momentum in recent years. The concept revolves around advocating for the rights, opportunities and overall well-being of women in various spheres of life. It involves ensuring that women enjoy the same rights, privileges and opportunities as men, thereby eliminating gender-based discrimination and inequality. Moreover, women's empowerment aims to topple the deeply embedded cultural conventions and gender stereotypes that restrict women's potential and assign them to submissive positions. It highlights how crucial it is to have a welcoming and secure atmosphere in which women feel free to voice their opinions, speak out and actively engage in choices that have an impact on their lives. Encouraging women's equality and empowerment benefits not just the women but also the society at large. Greater economic growth, a decrease in poverty and social well-being are the results of giving women equal opportunities and encouraging their active participation in society's progress. Furthermore, it helps break the intergenerational inequality cycle by providing future generations equitable opportunity, healthcare and education. Globally, women's empowerment and equality have been greatly aided by several projects, groups and organisations. They support gender-responsive policies, equal pay, stronger laws against violence and discrimination and venues that provide a voice to women. Even while there has been some progress, real gender equality and the empowerment of all women remain distant goals. Prejudices, biases and systemic impediments that impede advancement must be continually challenged at the individual, social and institutional levels. To create a more equitable, inclusive and affluent society, women's empowerment and equality are essential. We can build a society where everyone may prosper and contribute to the fullest extent possible by empowering women and guaranteeing them equal rights and opportunities. Women empowerment aims to challenge and change the traditional power dynamics that have historically marginalised women and hindered their progress. It advocates for women's right to make decisions and choices concerning their bodies, education, career and personal lives, while also advocating for equal access to resources, opportunities and justice. Women have encountered many difficulties and roadblocks in their quest for equality and empowerment throughout history. However, several groups, activists and movements have worked nonstop to advance women's rights and make important reforms. Women are now more often involved in decision-making roles and have better access to healthcare, education and career opportunities as a result of their initiatives. Many countries still experience prejudice and gender inequality despite advancements. As a result, raising awareness, pushing for legislative reforms and encouraging equality and women's empowerment at all levels are crucial. This calls for tackling societal expectations, prejudices and legislative restrictions that impede the advancement of women. Moreover, it is imperative to provide essential support networks, such as education, healthcare and employment prospects, to guarantee that women may fully realise their potential and assert their rights. The advancement and development of societies depend heavily on the equality and empowerment of women. Equal rights, resources and opportunities for women will enable us to create more equitable and welcoming communities that advance societal advancement. The traditionally male-dominated construction sector is changing radically as more women overcome gender stereotypes to provide their knowledge and abilities. In addition to being a question of equity, the shift in the construction industry towards gender diversity is strategically necessary for the long-term expansion and viability of the sector.

1.1 Empowerment via Economic and Educational Prospects

One of the most potent catalysts for women's empowerment is education. Women with access to high-quality education are more prepared to question social conventions and transcend conventional gender stereotypes. Moreover, the augmentation of women's agency is significantly dependent on economic empowerment. Societies may establish an atmosphere that supports women's economic success by granting them equal chances in the workforce, encouraging entrepreneurship and reducing the gender wage gap.

1.2 Modifying Cultural Storylines

Stereotypes and cultural norms support the continuation of discriminatory acts by maintaining gender inequality. It is essential to refute these myths and advance inclusion. Redefining cultural views regarding women is mostly the responsibility of the media, educational institutions and community leaders. Communities may aid in the elimination of gender-based discrimination by promoting an environment that values tolerance, understanding and equitable opportunity.

1.3 Legal Structures and Policy Measures

To reduce gender inequality, strong legislative frameworks and policy measures are essential. It is crucial to uphold laws that defend women's rights, guarantee employment equity and stop gender-based violence. Governments must seek to establish an atmosphere that actively advances gender equality while also defending women's rights in cooperation with civil society.

Modern Difficulties: Even with these developments, gender inequality still exists in modern culture. In addition to societal constraints that limit them to conventional jobs, women frequently experience income inequalities and low representation in leadership positions. Comprehensive solutions are urgently needed, as evidenced by problems like gender-based violence, poor healthcare and restricted access to reproductive rights. Discrimination affects women differently depending on criteria including ethnicity, class and sexual orientation. It also connects with other types of marginalisation.

1.4 Historical Background

Women have historically experienced structural marginalisation and discrimination, which has restricted their involvement in a variety of aspects of life. Women have struggled mightily for their rights ever since the suffragette campaigns of the late 19th and early 20th centuries and the following feminist waves. With landmarks like the ability to vote, obtain an education and enter the workforce, progress has been accomplished. Nonetheless, long-standing prejudices and patriarchal standards still prevent women from reaching their full potential.

1.5 The Shifting Landscape

There has been a discernible change in the industry's views towards gender diversity in recent years. In addition to taking on administrative responsibilities, more women are joining the construction industry as skilled workers, project managers, architects and engineers. Women's latent potential is progressively being recognised by the business, and programmes are being put in place to promote and encourage female participation.

Empowering Women in Construction: Developing an inclusive culture and breaking down systemic barriers are key to empowering women in the construction industry. Attracting and keeping female talent requires focused recruitment efforts, mentorship programmes and educational activities. Addressing problems like pay disparities, harassment in the workplace and discriminatory behaviours is also necessary to break ground and establish a work climate where women can flourish and make valuable contributions.

1.6 Benefits of Gender Diversity

There are several advantages to having more women in the construction industry. According to a wealth of research, diverse teams are more creative, productive and more suited to tackle challenging situations. The construction sector can increase its competitiveness in a fast-changing global market, improve decision-making processes and access a wider talent pool by adopting a diverse workforce.

1.7 Case Studies and Success Stories

Reading about women who have succeeded in the construction sector and studying case studies that highlight their successes may be inspirational and motivating. Citing businesses that have aggressively enacted gender-inclusive policies and seen successful results might offer insightful information on the most effective ways to empower women in the workplace. To sum up, advancing women's empowerment in the construction sector is a calculated step towards making the business more robust, creative and competitive as well as a question of equality. By tearing down past obstacles, enacting inclusive policies and sharing success stories, the construction sector can create an atmosphere where women feel empowered and can make a big contribution to its expansion and prosperity. To have an equitable and just society, women's empowerment and equality are essential. We can all benefit from better social, economic and political circumstances if we empower women. Women must have equal access to education and work opportunities for them to realise their full potential and make a positive contribution to society as a whole. To create a society that is inclusive and peaceful, it is also crucial to advance gender equality and abolish prejudice against women. It will take a team effort from individuals, governments and

organisations to confront and alter deeply rooted gender conventions and prejudices to achieve genuine women's empowerment and equality. We can only
establish a society that is equal and affluent for everyone if we value the rights,
voices and contributions of women.

2. EMPOWERING WOMEN IN CONSTRUCTION

Historically, men have dominated the construction sector, and women have faced
considerable obstacles to admission and promotion. Nonetheless, the necessity of
diversity and inclusivity in all spheres of society has resulted in an increasing
acknowledgement of the significance of empowering women in the construction
industry. Breaking gender stereotypes, establishing equal opportunities, offering
assistance and resources, encouraging leadership positions and cultivating an
inclusive work environment are just a few of the ways that women in construction
may be empowered. In addition to advancing gender equality, empowering
women in this sector opens up a large talent and skill pool, which helps the
construction sector grow. Even though women have come a long way in shattering stereotypes and joining the construction sector, there are still big obstacles
to overcome. For this reason, attempts are being undertaken to eliminate the
institutionalised prejudices and discriminatory practices that impede the
advancement of women in this industry. Governments, businesses and private
citizens are uniting to support programmes aimed at empowering women and
levelling the playing field for them in the construction industry. Establishing a
culture that promotes and supports women to seek jobs in construction is
essential to empowering women in the industry. It entails offering professional
development initiatives, training opportunities and mentorship programmes that
are specifically designed to meet the requirements of women. We can guarantee
women's success and provide them with the tools they need to prosper in the
construction sector by addressing their particular difficulties. To truly empower
people, workplace harassment and discrimination concerns must be addressed.
Women may confidently contribute their talents and ideas in a secure and
inclusive work environment, which encourages innovation and improves
industry performance overall. Furthermore, empowering women in leadership
roles in the construction sector may act as role models for the younger generation
of women and encourage them to follow professions in this area. By dismantling
barriers, fostering inclusive workplaces and offering equal opportunities, we can
harness the full potential of women in construction and build a brighter future for
the industry as a whole. Empowering women in construction is not just about

promoting gender equality; it's also a strategic move to drive innovation, diversity and sustainability within the industry. To empower women in the construction industry, it is necessary to address prejudice and bias based on gender, give them access to training and education, put work–life balance rules into place and promote inclusive and courteous workplace environments. Mentoring programmes, selective hiring and recruitment procedures and family-friendly incentives like paid parental leave are a few tactics that may be used to empower women (Padavic et al., 2020). Although women only make up 14% of the workforce in construction, the sector provides a variety of options for them, including management and leadership positions, research and development positions and hands-on skills. Still, there remain obstacles for women in the field to overcome, such as prejudices and a lack of knowledge about opportunities. By collaborating and interacting with colleges and high schools to host career fairs and employment possibilities, the project seeks to address these issues (Deltek, 2023). The aim is to enable women to excel in the profession by empowering them to ask questions, grow in confidence and shatter prejudices.

To develop a workforce that is more diverse and equitable, the project also emphasises how important it is for women to assist and mentor other women. The construction sector has historically been male-dominated, with very few women breaking through the restrictions in this historically masculine domain. But in recent decades, there has been a push for gender equality and a climate that supports women's empowerment in the construction industry. This book emphasises the value of women's empowerment in the construction industry, as well as the many obstacles they encounter and the associated solutions.

2.1 Significance of Women's Empowerment in Construction

2.1.1 Diversity and Innovation

A diverse group of people in the workplace would hence bring new perspectives and ideas to the work table. Making room for women in construction would, therefore, bring in a new kind of diversity and innovation.

2.1.2 Economic Growth

When women are involved in construction, more skills are given a chance to operate businesses and contribute towards economic growth. The general result of an increased workforce gives rise to more efficiency and effective levels of workforce productivity.

2.1.3 Equity and Social Development

Empowering women in construction is a means to get them equal. It defies the stereotypes to have social progress and progression towards a more inclusive and equitable society.

2.1.4 Gendered Stereotypes

Daily encounters include deep stereotypes and deep-rooted biases that often discourage the womenfolk from taking up careers in construction. Changing the perceptions in society is fundamental to breaking these barriers.

Culture in the Workplace: This has particularly made it difficult for women who seek to be part of the construction industry because of its traditionally masculine culture. For attracting and retaining female talent, an organisational culture that promotes inclusion is a necessary condition.

2.1.5 Under-Representation

The way women are represented in this form of leadership is one reason why most women are discouraged from venturing into the construction sector. This concept involves encouraging and nurturing women to such a form of leadership.

2.2 Methods of Women's Empowerment in Construction

2.2.1 Education and Training (Mentorship and Networking Promotion)

Continuing with educational programmes that could encourage little girls to study science, technology, engineering and mathematics (STEM) subjects could offer a likely foundation for the induction of women into construction. Positive reinforcement procedures may also be applicable.

Non-local multidisciplinary consulting institutes, education and collaboration-like institutions would work. From this perspective, it is, therefore, necessary to establish mentorship programmes and networking opportunities that can provide the necessary support and advice that are required to help women participants in the field deal with industry challenges and build themselves within the construction industry.

2.2.2 Advocacy for the Construction Industry

Advocacy of the cause of gender diversity in construction must be a part of industry organisations and associations. A united change to the mindset and welcoming women to join this industry will make a more conducive environment for welcoming women.

Empowering women in the construction industry is not just related to justice and equality issues but also a strategic move to arm the country with a more innovative and prosperous future. Thus, by facing the challenges presented by women and bridging them towards inclusivity, the potential for the construction industry workforce shall have no limits, and henceforth, it will be able to build a better future with no walls. In addition to promoting variety and creativity, empowering women in the construction sector is crucial for attaining gender equality. An inclusive workplace that embraces many viewpoints and ideas will result from a rise in the number of women working in the construction industry. Furthermore, encouraging female leadership in the construction sector might aid in addressing the present labour shortage that the sector is experiencing.

Construction businesses may enhance their workforce and fulfil the expanding industry needs by using the full potential of women and offering them equitable chances for training and career growth. Investing in the advancement of women in the building industry yields noteworthy economic advantages as well. Research has indicated that organisations with diverse workforces typically have superior productivity and profitability. Encouraging women to engage fully in the construction industry can result in higher project profitability, better project results and general economic growth. Moreover, empowering women in the building industry may benefit society as a whole. It can dispel preconceived notions about gender and show that women can succeed in sectors that have historically been dominated by males. This might contribute to the dismantling of obstacles and encourage females in later generations to work in the construction industry, therefore closing the gender gap and fostering more equality in society. It is advantageous for everyone when women are empowered in the construction sector. The sector gains from a more varied, inventive and successful workforce, while women benefit from equal chances and assistance for professional growth. The construction sector can fully realise gender equality by empowering women and removing obstacles while fostering diversity.

3. EQUITY AND OPPORTUNITIES IN CONSTRUCTION

Since the construction sector is in charge of creating and maintaining vital infrastructure, it has a big influence on how our cities and communities are shaped. Notwithstanding its significance, the industry has historically encountered obstacles to fairness and prospects. This pertains to the equitable allocation of resources, advantages and prospects to every person engaged in the construction industry, irrespective of their unique history or attributes.

To promote equity in the construction sector, it is necessary to guarantee that all people, irrespective of their gender, colour or socio-economic background, have equal access to opportunities, treatment and career progression. Fair hiring procedures, encouraging diversity and inclusion, paying equally for equal labour and fostering an inclusive workplace free from prejudice or discrimination are all examples of this. Furthermore, removing obstacles that can prevent people from entering and succeeding in the construction business is necessary to provide equitable chances. In the past, individuals of colour and women in particular have encountered structural barriers in their attempts to work in the construction industry. Through the removal of these obstacles and the advancement of inclusion, the construction sector may access a more diverse talent pool and improve productivity and creativity. Furthermore, it is both morally and financially necessary for the building industry to prioritise fairness and opportunities. Numerous studies have demonstrated that inclusive and diverse workplaces boost company outcomes, including profitability, cooperation, problem-solving skills and employee happiness. Construction businesses may create a work climate that benefits their employees and their financial line by embracing equity and possibilities. The relevance of fairness and opportunity has been increasingly recognised in the construction business in recent years.

To solve these problems and encourage diversity and inclusion in their workforce, several organisations and business leaders have begun putting these tactics into practice. This covers projects including training programmes to assist minority populations, mentorship programmes and focused recruiting campaigns. Still, a lot of work has to be done. Equity and chances must be given top priority as the construction sector develops to level the playing field for everyone. By doing this, we can guarantee that our construction projects represent the many needs and viewpoints of the communities they serve in addition to creating a more inclusive business. Eliminating obstacles that have traditionally kept women from entering and progressing in the construction industry is necessary to achieve gender equity and equitable opportunity in the sector. Important actions include encouraging fair hiring and remuneration procedures, giving women access to leadership positions and training and creating regulations that assist working parents in striking a work–life balance (Sang & Powell, 2012). Empirical data suggest that a broader increase in female participation leads to an overall culture inside the sector that is safer, more inventive and more productive. To advance equality and opportunity for women in the construction industry, several measures are recommended in the United Nations Development Programme (UNDP) study Breaking Ground: Empowering Women in the Construction Industry. Among these are the following:

3.1 Challenging Gender Stereotypes and Discrimination

Governments, businesses and organisations need to work together to challenge gender stereotypes and discrimination in the construction industry. This can be done by raising awareness of the issue, providing training on unconscious bias and implementing policies that promote gender equality.

3.2 Expanding Access to Training and Mentorship

Governments, businesses and organisations need to expand access to training and mentorship opportunities for women in the construction industry. This can be done by providing financial assistance, developing targeted training programmes and creating mentorship networks.

3.3 Promoting Work–Life Balance

Businesses and organisations must promote work–life balance for women in the construction industry. This can be done by offering flexible work arrangements, providing childcare support and creating a more supportive work culture.

The UNDP research suggests that in addition to these measures, companies and governments should encourage women-owned firms to be sourced from and encourage female entrepreneurship in the construction sector. Policies that support equal chances must be put into place and enforced within construction enterprises. Fair hiring practices, equitable compensation and anti-discrimination and harassment in the workplace guidelines must be upheld. Policies that support equal chances must be put into place and enforced within construction enterprises. The building industry has a significant impact on the built environment, yet equality and opportunity have always been problems for it. It is necessary to address issues like gender and racial inequalities, increase diversity and provide fair access to opportunities to foster a more inclusive and sustainable construction sector. This essay explores the importance of equality and opportunity in the construction industry, identifies key challenges and suggests ways to overcome them to create a more diverse and inclusive industry.

3.4 Opportunities and Equity Challenges

3.4.1 Gender Disparities

Historically, women have been under-represented in the construction sector. Women only make up a tiny portion of the workforce in construction-related industries, according to the National Association of Women in Construction (NAWIC). Stereotypes, a lack of representation and gender prejudice in the recruiting and promotion procedures are frequently blamed for this gender gap.

3.4.2 Racial and Ethnic Disparities

In the construction industry, minority groups – African Americans, Hispanics and other ethnic groups – face disadvantages in terms of employment and promotion. The persistence of inequality may be aided by the absence of diversity in positions of leadership and possibilities for professional advancement.

3.4.3 Educational Barriers

People wishing to work in the construction business may encounter obstacles due to a lack of access to high-quality education and training programmes. Ensuring that all individuals have equal opportunity to pursue a profession in construction requires addressing these educational inequalities.

3.5 Techniques for Encouraging Opportunities and Equity

3.5.1 Initiatives for Diversity and Inclusion

Building firms ought to put these into action and aggressively support them. These initiatives may include mentorship programmes, focused recruitment tactics and chances for minority groups to advance their leadership.

3.5.2 Education and Training Programmes

It is imperative to make investments in educational initiatives that offer inclusive, easily accessible training to anyone aspiring to work in the construction industry. Partnerships between academic institutions, community organisations and industry stakeholders can aid in closing the gap and paving the way for diverse talent.

3.5.3 Equitable Hiring Procedures

Construction firms must implement impartial and equitable hiring procedures. Unconscious biases can be reduced by using blind recruiting procedures, in which candidates are assessed based on their qualifications and abilities rather than their personal history.

3.5.4 Supportive Workplace Culture

It is critical to cultivate a culture at work that appreciates inclusivity and diversity. Businesses should establish support networks, offer continuous diversity training and take proactive measures to resolve any incidences of harassment or discrimination.

3.5.5 Community Engagement

Construction businesses may better understand and handle the particular difficulties encountered by various demographic groups by establishing connections with local communities. Through cooperation and understanding, this method helps to create a more diverse industry.

The long-term viability and sustainability of the construction sector depend on achieving equity and opportunity. The construction industry can develop a more resilient and dynamic workforce by addressing gender and racial imbalances, fostering diversity and inclusion and granting equitable access to chances for education and professional growth. Building a construction sector that represents the variety of the communities it serves is a shared duty of legislators, educators and leaders in the business. To foster inclusion, diversity and equitable access to resources and opportunities for all people, regardless of background, equality and opportunity in the construction business, is essential. Construction organisations may foster an inclusive atmosphere that values and supports employees from diverse demographic groups by implementing fair recruiting, training, promotion and compensation policies. Improving labour diversity in the construction sector can result from equal opportunity policies, which have been shown to boost innovation, creativity and general corporate success. Supporting minority-owned companies and contractors may also solve past injustices and promote economic prosperity. Employers and legislators must work together to remove obstacles that keep under-represented groups from joining and growing in the construction industry. Targeted training programmes, mentorship programmes, apprenticeships and laws that support equitable access to resources and contracts can all help achieve this. All things considered, putting fairness and possibilities first in the construction industry is not simply a question of social justice but also economic necessity. An open and diverse construction sector may foster innovation, promote sustainable growth and more accurately reflect the community it serves.

4. FEMALE CONTRIBUTION TO THE CONSTRUCTION INDUSTRY

In the construction sector, women are contributing significantly as engineers, project managers, executives, researchers and tradesmen, among other roles. Their involvement improves the field's creativity, output and teamwork (Ahuja, 2002). Still, there are misconceptions that building is 'men's work'. Ongoing efforts must be made to acknowledge and appreciate the vital contributions women contribute to the industry. Women have historically been notably under-represented in the construction business, which has generally been controlled by males. Nonetheless, there is a growing recognition of the significance of women in this field.

This book further examines how many women are now employed in the construction sector, the difficulties they encounter and the possibilities that exist. It also talks about how important it is to support diversity and create an inclusive workplace in the construction industry. Though historically thought to be dominated by males, the number of women working in the construction business has significantly increased in recent years. Women have defied expectations and surmounted obstacles to make extraordinary contributions that have revolutionised the building sector. Their involvement has increased the workforce and brought in a variety of viewpoints, abilities and talents, which has significantly increased growth and innovation in the industry. A significant element of female involvement in the construction sector is the rise in female employment in professions that have historically been filled by males, such as engineers, architects, contractors and project managers. These women have performed admirably in their positions, dispelling the myth that some vocations are only appropriate for males. Women have made it possible for a great number of others to follow in their footsteps by shattering these restrictions based on gender. In addition, women in the construction industry have shown to be outstanding leaders and have been crucial players in decision-making. Within the industry, their capacity to create winning ideas, identify creative solutions and manage projects effectively has been acknowledged and praised. As a result, more women are being given leadership roles and allowed to influence the direction the construction sector will take. Beyond the workforce, women contribute in other ways to the construction sector. Significant contributions from a large number of women have also been made to research, development and the use of sustainable building techniques. They have introduced novel viewpoints on ecologically friendly construction methods, energy-efficient designs and sustainable building materials.

The construction industry has become more environmentally sensitive as a result of the significant role women have played in fighting for greener and more sustainable practices within the sector. In addition, women have made progress in encouraging inclusion and diversity in the field. Their proactive participation in groups and associations has opened doors for networking events, mentorship programmes and campaigns to increase the number of women in the construction industry. Due to these initiatives, there are now more voices in the sector, which has made it fairer and more inclusive so that everyone may prosper and share their talents and ideas. It is impossible to undervalue the contributions made by women in the building sector. The industry has changed as a result of their greater presence, leadership positions, creative ideas and dedication to sustainability. Through shattering pre-conceptions, advocating for diversity and advancing inclusiveness, women have brought about a more progressive and vibrant construction sector that values their indispensable contributions. Gender diversity in the construction business has long been lacking, with women making up a minuscule portion of the workforce.

Though slowly, gender equality in the building and manufacturing sectors is nevertheless improving. The National Kitchen & Bath Association's consultant economist, Manuel Gutierrez, reports that women now make up 13.3% of construction workers and 28.6% of manufacturing workers (Karen, 2021). Even while the proportion of women joining the construction business has increased significantly – nearly twice as much as it did during the 1970s – the number of female workers has only increased by 1.7 percentage points over the previous 30 years (Karen, 2021).

In the construction industry, specialty trades accounted for 59% of employment, and women held 569,000, or 12.1%, of those occupations in 2020. A closer look at the specialist trades reveals that women held 13.4% of the positions in building/finishing (including finish carpentry), up 3.1 percentage points since 1990. Building equipment trades came in second, with women holding 9.7% of the occupations in this sector (1.3% increase) and building foundations at 12.8% (1.4% gain).

Notwithstanding this under-representation, women's participation in the construction sector is crucial to the expansion and prosperity of the sector. By stressing the value of gender diversity and the need to foster a more inclusive atmosphere, this book seeks to raise awareness of the contribution made by women to the construction sector.

4.1 Current State of Female Participation in the Construction Industry

As of 2023, women make up only about 1.25% of the construction workforce in the United States. While the number of women in the industry is gradually increasing, they are still significantly under-represented in trade and executive positions (BigRentz, 2024). The under-representation of women in the construction industry is a global issue, as evidenced by the low percentage of female board members in UK construction firms.

4.2 Challenges Faced by Women in the Construction Industry

Women in the construction industry encounter various challenges, including gender stereotypes, harassment and a lack of access to training and career advancement opportunities. The misconception that construction jobs are primarily physical has also contributed to the underutilisation of women's skills in the industry.

4.3 Opportunities for Women in the Construction Industry

Despite the challenges, women can pursue diverse roles in the construction sector, such as procurement, surveying, health and safety and executive positions. The industry is projected to experience steady growth, creating new job opportunities, and women are increasingly being recruited to bring their unique skill sets to the field.

4.4 Importance of Promoting Diversity and Fostering an Inclusive Environment

Promoting diversity and inclusivity in the construction industry is crucial for attracting a broad range of talent and expertise. Partnering with women-owned construction companies and ensuring equal employment opportunities are among the measures that can lead to increased success and benefit both contractors and the communities they serve.

The rise of women in the construction industry is reshaping its standard for success, and their participation is vital for creating an equal and diverse workforce. Despite the existing barriers, the number of women in the industry is expected to continue rising, presenting new opportunities for female professionals. By addressing gender stereotypes, promoting equal opportunities and fostering an inclusive environment, the construction industry can benefit from the valuable contributions of women. The crucial role that women play in the construction sector has been growing over the past several years. In an area that has historically been controlled by males, women have shown themselves to be extremely knowledgeable and capable. Their participation has given rise to a variety of viewpoints, enhanced productivity and heightened creativity in the sector. In addition, women bring special talents including excellent problem-solving, attention to detail and communication skills that are crucial to the success of building projects. Still, there remains work to be done to advance gender equality and give women in leadership roles similar chances. It is important to keep up the efforts to assist the professional growth of women in the construction sector and to inspire more of them to seek jobs in the field.

5. THE UNSEEN STRENGTH OF WOMEN IN CONSTRUCTION

Women frequently do crucial but underappreciated administrative and support jobs behind the scenes with machines and building sites. In addition to
handling IT requirements, they purchase supplies, maintain schedules, get
permissions and manage payroll (Tippett, 2018). Although it has long been
believed that males predominate in the construction sector, women have been
quietly breaking down barriers and making important contributions, despite
this stereotype. Women have been progressively making their mark in the
construction business throughout the years, demonstrating that they have
certain abilities and traits that are priceless to the sector.

The perseverance, determination and flexibility of women in the construction industry have been astounding, despite cultural expectations and gender
preconceptions. They have broken through barriers and glass ceilings,
demonstrating that strength can take on many different forms, including
mental, emotional and physical strength. The capacity of women in construction to promote teamwork and cultivate long-lasting connections is one of
their unsung talents. Their innate ability to empathise and communicate
effectively makes them excellent at building strong teams and bridging gaps
between various stakeholders. Women foster variety and contribute new
viewpoints to projects by advocating for an inclusive culture, which boosts
creativity and problem-solving abilities. The construction business greatly
benefits from the invisible power of women's attention to detail and accuracy.
Their excellent attention to detail guarantees that every facet of a project is
investigated in detail and carried out to the highest standard, regardless of the
field – design, project management or quality control. This attention to detail
guarantees the completion of projects that meet or even surpass expectations
and helps prevent expensive mistakes. In addition, women in construction
have outstanding organising abilities. They are adept at handling many
responsibilities at once, adhering to strict deadlines and overcoming challenging logistical situations. Construction projects are completed successfully
in part because of their capacity to remain calm and concentrated under
pressure.

The versatility and problem-solving skills of women in the construction
industry are another important but sometimes underappreciated asset. Because
building sites are dynamic places with ever-changing conditions, women's
quick thinking and agility enable them to adapt successfully to unforeseen
problems. Their capacity for creative problem-solving and unconventional
thinking not only improves construction processes' efficiency but also makes
the workplace safer. In conclusion, women's perseverance, teamwork,

attention to detail, organisational skills, flexibility and problem-solving talents are the overlooked strengths of the construction industry. These advantages have a major positive impact on the development and prosperity of the construction sector. Given that women's potential is still unsurpassed and that their contributions will continue to influence the direction of construction, we must acknowledge and value the tremendous influence that women have in this industry. To fully value women's efforts in construction, it is important to acknowledge the important supporting roles that they play. It is imperative to implement policies that guarantee fair compensation, benefits and career growth prospects. Women are remarkably strong, even though this is sometimes overlooked. Recognising the unsung power of women in construction is an important issue. Building projects benefit from the distinct viewpoints, problem-solving abilities, and meticulous attention to detail that women provide. They are an invaluable addition to any construction team because of their capacity for multitasking and productive collaboration. Historically, the construction sector has been predominantly male-dominated, with a notable under-representation of women in different professions. Nonetheless, the important contributions made by women in this field are becoming more widely acknowledged. By examining the existing level of female engagement, the difficulties they face and the possibilities available to them, this chapter seeks to highlight the unsung power of women in the construction industry. It also highlights how important it is to advance inclusiveness and diversity in the construction sector. Women have hidden strength that is a powerful force. Men have been perceived as occupying the construction sector for a substantial length of time. The noise produced by hammers and large machinery is frequently connected to men. However, a quiet revolution has been taking place lately: an increasing number of women are employed in the construction sector. The unheralded force of women in the construction industry is transforming the landscape and busting long-held misconceptions, even though they may not be as numerous as men.

5.1 Breaking Stereotypes

Historically, the construction industry has been linked to toughness and physical strength, traits that are frequently stereotypically associated with males. The entry of women into the construction industry, however, dispels these myths. In addition to their physical strength, women in construction also contribute their mental toughness, meticulousness and good communication abilities.

5.2 Diversity of Skill

Women in construction add to the industry's wide skill base. Diverse teams – including ones with a gender – tend to be more creative and effective, according to research. The diverse problem-solving techniques and innovative viewpoints that women frequently provide to building projects improve their overall effectiveness and success.

5.3 Leadership Roles

The growing number of women in leadership positions in the construction industry is an example of the invisible strength of these workers. Women have proven to be capable of leading teams, making important choices and effectively managing challenging projects. Research suggests that organisations with diverse leadership teams – including women – perform better overall and are more profitable.

5.4 Handling Personnel Shortages

A recurring issue in the construction sector is the lack of trained personnel. Women's participation reduces this problem by providing access to a larger talent pool. In addition to advancing equality, encouraging women to engage in construction also increases the number of workers in the sector.

5.5 Workplace Dynamics Are Changing

As more women enter the construction industry, workplace dynamics are changing. Businesses are realising how important it is to provide a welcoming and encouraging atmosphere for both male and female employees. Increased work happiness, staff retention and general productivity are all impacted by this cultural transformation.

The construction business, which has historically resisted change, is being transformed by the invisible strength of women. As more and more women break down barriers, their influence on the construction industry is not limited to physical labour; it also includes leadership, creativity and a more welcoming workplace environment. In addition to promoting gender equality, recognising and honouring the achievements of women in the construction sector is a calculated step towards building a more robust and resilient sector. Building on the many assets that women contribute to the business, the construction sector can lay the groundwork for a more prosperous and sustainable future.

The unsung potential of women in the construction industry is a strong force. Though construction has historically been an industry dominated by males, women have been breaking down barriers, dispelling myths and demonstrating their competence and ability in a variety of construction jobs. Their tenacity, fortitude and meticulousness provide them priceless resources for the sector. Despite being frequently disregarded, women's contributions to the construction industry are essential to the growth and development of projects. To build a more inclusive and varied business, it is imperative that society acknowledge, value and promote the invisible power of women in the construction sector. Women may continue to offer their special skills and views to the construction business, making it more sustainable and prosperous for everyone, by advancing education, breaking down gender barriers and providing equitable opportunities.

6. EMPOWERING WOMEN TO SHAPE THE BUILT WORLD

Since construction affects almost every element of life, including the opinions and views of women produces structures and infrastructure that better serve whole communities. Women are empowered to assume leadership positions where they may use their skills and perspectives to influence the built environment through mentoring programmes, inclusive workplace practices and access to education and training (Worrall et al., 2010). In addition to being a question of gender equality, empowering women is also a wise financial move. In addition to improving development results for the next generation and increasing economic output, greater gender equality may also increase the representation of institutions and policies. Labour, the economy and sustainability are just a few areas of society where women's empowerment has a big influence. Women are making significant contributions to a wide range of areas in today's fast-paced and changing world, shattering preconceptions and demonstrating their worth in all spheres of life. This is also true of the built environment industry, which includes engineering, construction, architecture and urban planning. But despite all of their accomplishments, women are still under-represented in this field and face many obstacles.

A crucial initiative to level the playing field and provide women equal chances to succeed in their fields is empowering women to design the built environment. It acknowledges the enormous contribution that many viewpoints and experiences make to the creation and design of physical locations as well as to the general innovation and expansion of the industry. The first steps towards empowering women are education and removing obstacles that prevent them from pursuing professions in the built environment. Important first efforts towards achieving more equitable representation in the industry include fostering inclusion in educational institutions, providing mentorship and funding opportunities and encouraging young females to pursue their interests in STEM professions. Creating a welcoming and inclusive work environment is another way to empower women in the built environment. It entails confronting institutionalised prejudice and eliminating gender-based preconceptions that have endured for many years. Organisations may foster an atmosphere where women feel appreciated, acknowledged and enabled to realise their whole potential by advocating for equitable recruiting procedures, equal compensation and chances for career progression. Celebrating the accomplishments of women who have already made major contributions to the built environment sector is another aspect of empowerment. By showcasing these trailblazers, we may encourage and motivate aspiring female professionals with their successes, demonstrating that they, too, have the power to influence and change the built environment. By empowering women, we can close the gender gap in the built environment industry and take advantage of their enormous ability, creativity and skill set. Together, we can create an inclusive industry, actively promote women and foster their growth so that the built environment is not only visually beautiful and useful but also reflects the many viewpoints and experiences of all people. The effects of empowering women are seen in several international development initiatives. For example, women's empowerment in the workforce has improved the lives of these women in Egypt, India and Bangladesh, but it has also highlighted the need for more safety. In a similar vein, programmes like Cocoa Life have shown how women can accelerate change and magnify effect in all spheres of sustainability. Empowering women can result in more inclusive and sustainable development in the context of the built environment. The built environment can benefit from the many viewpoints and creative solutions that women's involvement in urban planning, design, building and engineering can provide. More ecologically friendly and gender-inclusive environments may be created as a result of this. It is crucial to have laws and programmes in place that encourage gender equality, equal access to education and training and chances for women to participate in decision-making processes to enable women to shape the built environment. To further ensure success, assessing the results of these initiatives and creating precise action plans for women's empowerment are essential. The ideals, growth and progress of civilisation are only reflected in the constructed environment. Since their beginning, the design and building sectors have been controlled by men, with women's potential being overlooked in their advancement. Nonetheless, it is becoming more and more apparent that women must be given the authority to lead change in the built environment. This book examines the value of women's empowerment in the fields of engineering, architecture and construction as well as how this may translate into advantages for the sector from a cultural standpoint.

6.1 The Situation at Hand

For quite a long time until fairly recently, career disparities in the built environment were pretty huge between the men's courses and those of women. Besides, gender stereotypes, unequal opportunities and lack of representation in roles of leadership have played a greater role in the under-representation of women in these industries. According to a recent report by the National Association of Women in Construction, only a fraction of the construction-related workforce is female.

6.2 Empowering Women Architects

Empowering women in architecture therefore requires breaking these ceilings and creating an all-inclusive atmosphere that inspires diversity. Architecture is paramount to the physical world with ideas from different backgrounds giving rise to sustainable and creative designs. For example, American Institute of Architects (AIA) is the Equity in Architecture Commission that aims to bridge the gender gap in the architecture profession by advocating for equal opportunities and representation.

6.3 Empowering Women in Engineering

The engineering profession, including fields such as civil engineering and structural design, has been traditionally male-dominated, and women's participation in the field has remained relatively low. However, organisations seek to build their strength with the Society of Women Engineers (SWE), which aims to help women pursue and succeed in their engineering careers. Promoting the exploration of STEM education in girls at their tender age is an essential consideration for breaking gender barriers in engineering and ensuring that there is an increased female participation in this field.

6.4 Strategies on How to Empower Women Who Are Working in Construction

Certainly, since the construction industry has been male-dominated and like other industries, it has lagged on the aspect of gender balancing in every way. Empowerment of women in the sector of construction would mean offering them equal opportunities, defying stereotypes and framing a culture within the workplace where differences are welcomed. Some of the organisations that have come up with encouraging and championed policies supporting the promotion of women in the construction area include NAWIC, which emerged to be of great help.

6.5 Reasons for Supporting Women's Promotion in the Built World

Innovation and Creativity: Different perspectives that diverse people between the teams hold can be merged to generate highly innovative outcomes in design and construction.

Enhanced Decision-Making: Research has been conducted and holds that the best decisions come from diverse teams. The responses and experiences can be gained for the built environment by a wider look at the designing of spaces through empowered women in leadership.

Workplace Satisfaction: Developing workplaces inclusive of valuing diversity would result in higher levels of satisfaction from jobs and reduce the attrition rate of employees, thus creating an industry that is stable and productive.

Social and Economic Impact: Disempowering women in the built world not only negatively impacts but also towards the overall economic development through the underutilisation of talent.

Empowering women to shape the built world is tantamount to a social justice agenda and, at a more pragmatic level, one that underpins the human development agenda. We are, therefore, able to unlock the full potential of diverse talents and create a built environment that genuinely reflects the richness of human experience by eroding these barriers and creating equal opportunities with inclusive environments.

Gaining the ability of women to influence the built environment is essential to building a more inventive, ecological and egalitarian future. The amount of skill, innovation and many views that women contribute to various fields may benefit society by addressing the obstacles they confront and encouraging their active involvement. In addition to being a question of social fairness, achieving gender parity in the built environment is strategically necessary for the growth and improvement of our international communities. Encouraging women to take charge of the built environment is a calculated step towards societal advancement as well as gender equality. Women may offer their special views and abilities to the built environment, resulting in improved design, innovation and sustainable development, by breaking down barriers and fostering equitable opportunities. Furthermore, empowering women in this field may lead to better public spaces, infrastructure and urban planning that accommodate the interests and requirements of all people, resulting in more liveable and inclusive communities. Furthermore, the constructed environment may gain from varied thinking, cooperation and more efficient problem-solving by actively including women in leadership roles and decision-making processes. In the end, giving women the authority to influence the built environment benefits everyone involved by advancing gender equality, spurring creativity and improving the general standard of living in our cities.

7. REDEFINING ROLES FOR WOMEN TO TRIUMPH IN CONSTRUCTION

The demographics of the construction business have significantly changed in recent years, as more women are breaking down old barriers and joining the sector. There is an increasing need to redefine the roles that women may play in this traditionally male-dominated area of construction as more and more women show their experience, abilities and love for the industry. Construction has always been thought of as a physically hard job that is best suited for males. These ideas, however, are dispelling themselves as more and more women defy expectations and demonstrate their proficiency in every facet of the field. Women are thriving in the construction industry by contributing distinctive viewpoints, creative ideas and strong leadership to a range of fields including design, engineering, project management and skilled crafts. Promoting inclusiveness and equitable chances is one of the most important parts of redefining roles so that women may succeed in the construction industry. Companies are increasingly placing a high priority on diversity and advocating for gender equality in the sector as they realise that gender diversity not only creates a more harmonious and fulfilling work environment but also boosts productivity. This change is fostering an environment where women may flourish and reach their greatest potential. A further aspect of redefining roles in construction is dispelling stereotypes that women aren't as capable or strong enough to excel in particular fields. As it is, women are demonstrating their abilities in several jobs that were previously thought to be exclusive to males. The industry is gradually removing these stereotypes and levelling the playing field for everyone by emphasising credentials, abilities and experience above gender. In the construction industry, women are also actively engaging in decision-making processes and assuming leadership roles. Women are making their impact at every level, from CEOs and company owners to project managers and site supervisors. In addition to improving the performance of the business, their distinct viewpoints and managerial skills are motivating and inspiring more women to seek prosperous careers in construction. All things considered, the redefining of women's positions in construction is evidence of the industry's progress. In the construction industry, ability, expertise and devotion are winning out against gender prejudices as obstacles and stereotypes continue to be dismantled. In an increasingly gender-neutral world where women continue to be indispensable in defining the built environment, the industry is embracing equal opportunity and inclusivity and acknowledging the achievements of women. It is necessary to refute and question preconceived notions regarding the roles and talents of women in the construction industry. Women may excel in trades like welding, electrical work and heavy equipment operation with the right training and support (Eskridge & Carini, 2017). According to Sang and Powell (2012), women are still under-represented in professions including project management, engineering and architecture. Companies must re-evaluate the prejudices ingrained in the policies and culture of the workplace. Although males have historically held the majority of positions in the construction sector, there is a growing understanding that for women to succeed in this area, roles must be redefined. Reaching the target of 25% female workforce in construction by 2025 is essential to building a sector in which women may participate fully. The number of women employed in construction occupations has significantly increased, despite the obstacles and prejudices that women in the sector still face. These women contribute to the sector in a variety of ways, ranging from skilled workers to on-site supervisors. Redefining the construction business and fostering an inclusive atmosphere requires recognising women's accomplishments and advocating for gender equality. Experiences in Egypt, India and Bangladesh demonstrate that empowering women in the workforce has a favourable effect on development programmes globally. Gender prejudices must be addressed, equal training and professional growth opportunities must be offered and women's presence in leadership roles within the sector must be encouraged. By doing this, the workforce in the construction industry will be more skilled and diversified, which will boost productivity and creativity. Men predominate in the construction industry, with women being significantly under-represented. Sociological data have further supported this; however, as diversity and inclusion issues in society become more widely acknowledged, women's positions in the construction sector need to be re-evaluated to focus on their realistic outcomes. Men have historically had a dominant position in the construction sector, and women frequently face major obstacles to success. Nonetheless, a more inventive, varied and prosperous construction industry may result from rethinking roles for women and appreciating their special abilities. This book indicates the difficulties faced by women in the construction sector, the advantages of increasing gender diversity and tactics for enabling and assisting women to succeed in this sector.

7.1 Challenges Faced by Women in Construction

Women working in construction have long been faced with numerous hurdles that include stereotypes, gender bias, as well a lack of mentorship opportunities. The notion that construction is physically hard and male-dominated has set forth a lot in the recruitment as well as retention of women in construction. Additionally, due to the lack of female role models and mentors, these women in construction are likely to suffer isolation or have limited career advancement opportunities.

7.2 Benefits Associated With Increased Gender Diversification in Construction

Increased innovation and creativity as well as improvement in organisational performance have been noted as the consequences of diversity and inclusion in the workplace. Since the inclusion of women and their perspectives, experiences and ability to contribute to managerial and technical problem-solving is likely to lead to diversities in making decisions, construction projects may have a considerable benefit from including them. It also allows construction organisations to attract the best available talent and increase satisfaction among their employees, improving retention rates as well.

7.3 Strategies to Empower Women in Construction

Education and Training Programmes: The provision should be made for educational schemes that target girls and young women to opt for STEM subjects. Stipends and training programmes focusing on the entry of women into the construction industry would help cope with skill gaps and increase the participation of women in the industry.

Mentorship and Networking: It may be necessary to develop mentorship programmes where older women give guidance and support to young women newly joining the construction industry. To illustrate, therefore, mentorship should also entail the creation of both formal and informal networking opportunities that enable women to form professional connections and get access to resources required for career setting up.

Promoting Inclusive Policies: Have in place measures that promote gender equality including equal pay, flexibility in work arrangements in terms of working hours and family-friendly benefits. Measures promoting a supportive and inclusive working environment are key to the attraction and retention of suitably qualified women in the industry.

Breaking Stereotypes: The elimination and challenge of that gender stereotype within the construction industry is inevitable. Media as well as general public awareness campaigns promoting the success stories of women within construction supported by industry programmes will help in altering perceptions and ultimately get more women to take up careers within construction.

Not simply as a matter of social fairness but also as a strategic necessity for the construction industry's success, redefining the position of women will need to be addressed. Effectively handling rigidity, guaranteeing diversity and implementing policies to promote this kind of workforce would provide possibilities where the construction industry might profit from a larger, more gender-ready labour pool. This calls for collaboration between those running educational institutions, business leaders and legislators. Embracing diversity will not only help women succeed in the industry as a whole, but it will also spur innovation, development and sustainability initiatives in the construction industry as a whole. A more inventive, successful and inclusive sector of the construction industry may result from redefining positions for women and valuing varied talent. Construction companies may use the entire potential of their workforce by appreciating women's distinct abilities and views, empowering them through techniques of empowerment and encouraging them to seek non-traditional professions. To bring about victory and success for women in the construction industry as well as for the sector overall, roles for women in the sector must be redefined. It's no secret that males have historically controlled the construction business, but by embracing women and giving them equal opportunity, the sector can access a huge reservoir of talent, views and abilities. Construction businesses can foster a more diverse and inclusive workforce that will enhance creativity, productivity and profitability by dismantling gender preconceptions and prejudices. Construction projects may benefit immensely from the special skills that women bring to the table, including excellent communication, collaborative problem-solving and attention to detail. To overcome the obstacles and difficulties that women frequently encounter while seeking jobs in construction, measures such as bettering hiring and retention procedures, giving flexible work schedules and equal compensation and career growth chances should be taken. Talented women will be attracted to and retained by construction businesses if a welcoming and inclusive atmosphere is established, allowing them to flourish in their positions. In addition, initiatives for education and training should be created to empower and encourage women to work in the construction sector by giving them the credentials and know-how required for success. A major factor in drawing and keeping women in construction jobs is the promotion of STEM education for females, apprenticeship programmes and mentorship opportunities. It is the duty of governmental organisations, trade groups and building firms to aggressively advance diversity and gender equality in the industry. It is crucial to put laws and policies into place that support gender parity and guarantee women in the construction industry receive equitable treatment and opportunity. In addition to being a question of social justice and equality, redefining positions for women in the construction sector is also a calculated step that will support the business's long-term viability. The construction industry may advance and gain from the many skills and viewpoints that women bring to the table by using women's potential and fostering an inclusive atmosphere.

8. BUILDING A BETTER FUTURE FOR WOMEN IN CONSTRUCTION A MORE EQUITABLE AND INCLUSIVE

Because of the historical male dominance in the construction sector, it is difficult for women to enter and excel in this area. Nonetheless, a lot of work has been done recently to improve the future for women in the construction industry to create a more inclusive and fairer sector. Addressing the numerous obstacles that women encounter in the construction industry and fostering an atmosphere that encourages gender parity and equal opportunity are essential to building a better future for women in this sector. This entails dispelling prejudices and preconceptions, creating welcoming work environments, encouraging women in leadership and mentoring roles and giving them access to the tools and education they need to be successful. The enormous potential that women bring to the construction industry is one of the main arguments in favour of concentrating on gender equality in the sector. Construction businesses may benefit from a broader range of talent, views and skills by diversifying their staff. This can enhance creativity, productivity and problem-solving abilities. Initiatives and organisations supporting women's entry, promotion and leadership in the construction industry have been formed to create a more equal and inclusive future for women in the sector. These programmes seek to close the gender wage gap, enhance women's work–life balance, give them access to apprenticeships and training and connect them with mentors and other women. Beyond workplace measures, however, is a better future for women in construction. It also entails interacting with educational institutions, promoting construction as a career option for young women and dispelling myths that deter women from seeking these positions. We can not only provide women the chance to succeed in this business but also help the construction industry as a whole, by constructing a more equal and inclusive future for them. It is a crucial step in promoting gender equality and building a society in which everyone can fully utilise their abilities contribute their skills and talents and have equal access to opportunities. A courteous, harassment-free work site culture; access to education and training; hiring and promotion procedures that minimise prejudice; and workplace regulations that support flexibility and work–life balance are just a few of the many areas where the construction industry demands persistent efforts. As a consequence, the construction industry will grow stronger and more inventive, making the most of every worker's ability to create a brighter future (Ahuja, 2002). Although historically the construction business has been controlled by males, there is a rising awareness of the need to establish a more welcoming atmosphere for women. The 25% female workforce in construction must be reached by 2025 to guarantee women's full participation in the sector. The climate for women in construction is getting better, as seen by the notable rise in the number of women entering the field and achieving success in a variety of jobs, including skilled workers and on-site supervisors. Although there has been improvement, there are still issues that women in the construction industry must deal with, including stereotypes, gender prejudice and under-representation in leadership roles. Nonetheless, more women are being able to hold roles and support the growth of the construction industry thanks to the industry's growing gender equality. It is crucial to keep reinventing the sector, honouring women's accomplishments and combating gender prejudices and stereotypes to create a brighter future for women in the construction business. By adopting this, the building industry can foster a more inclusive and friendly work environment for women, which will result in a workforce that is more diversified and well-qualified. Because men predominate in the construction sector, women's participation in related jobs has lagged well behind. Employers are currently making significant progress in establishing a fair work environment for women in the business. This book shows the obstacles that women face, the efforts being made to promote inclusion and suggestions for improving the future for both present and future women working in the construction industry.

8.1 Challenges Facing Women in Construction

How they entered and what history they have in the industry stack up to significant complexities. Some of these barriers include gender stereotyping, under-representation, unequal opportunity to progress within the workforce and sometimes unwelcome culture.

8.2 Inclusivity Campaigns

Over the last couple of years, several campaigns have been initiated to look into countering gender inequality that is within the construction sector. For example, two influential bodies include the NAWIC, which work to provide support, networking opportunities, as well as mentorship for such women in construction (NAWIC, 2021). Furthermore, construction companies are taking part in diversity and inclusion programmes that facilitate changing the perception that construction sites are for men only into ones where everyone is welcomed regardless of gender.

8.3 Better Future Strategies

Education and Training: There is also an emphasis on the need to interest women in the construction industry at a tender age. Schools could hold programmes that help remove stereotypes for any given field, especially in construction, with a bid to encourage career opportunities for women in construction. Outreach efforts could also incorporate showing the different roles available in the industry.

8.3.1 Mentorship Programmes

There can be mentorship programmes designed in construction firms to guide women along their career path as well as constant support. This way, mentorship improves their careers and gives them confidence when working in construction companies.

8.3.2 Equal Opportunities

Companies should be able to go out of their way to ensure that equal opportunities for both genders are promoted in hiring, promotions and even assigning jobs or projects. A merit-based environment whereby decisions are arrived at transparently should be helpful to get rid of any kind of gender bias.

8.3.3 Workplace Culture and Inclusivity

To first retain and attract female talent, the workplace culture must be inclusive. Companies should invest in diversity training, and anti-discrimination legislation, and create a platform where everyone feels valued and respected by every other individual.

8.3.4 Flexible Work Arrangements

Offering flexible work arrangements such as remote working and flexibility in the working hours go a long way in mitigating some of the challenges that women face in their effort to balance work engagements and family life. It will, therefore, require collective responsibility from industry players, educational institutions and policymakers to work for a bright future for women in construction. Looking at the difficulties and challenges faced by women, promoting inclusiveness and working on strategic plans would possibly change the construction sector into a highly competitive and inclusive business world. Embracing a workforce that mirrors the richness of human diversity will not only benefit women but also boost innovation, creativity and overall success. It is a perfect time to build a future where women will be able to flourish and will contribute remarkably to the growth and sustainability of the construction sector. It is imperative to create a more fair and inclusive construction business to improve the future of women in the field. It is possible to attract and keep skilled women in all construction professions by tearing down gender prejudices and confronting social misconceptions. Giving women access to high-quality education and training programmes will help them get the knowledge and abilities needed to succeed in the construction industry. For women to have equal opportunity in construction jobs, discriminatory rules must be removed and inclusive hiring procedures must be put in place. Businesses and leaders in the field must place a high priority on workplace diversity and cultivate a welcoming atmosphere that recognises the contributions of women. In addition, networking and mentoring programmes tailored to women in construction may provide them with the assistance and direction they need to progress in their professions. We can create a more fair and inclusive construction sector and empower women by proactively addressing gender inequities and maximising their potential for success.

BIBLIOGRAPHY

Ahuja, V. (2002). Women in the construction workplace. *Construction Management & Economics*, 20(8), 617–623.

American Institute of Architects (AIA). (2022). Equity in architecture commission. https://www.aia.org/resources/7753642-equity-in-architecture-commission

AON. Rethinking women in construction. https://www.aon.com/industry-insights/rethinking-women-in-construction

BigRentz. Think big blog. Women in construction: The state of the industry in 2024. https://www.bigrentz.com/blog/women-construction#:~:text=A%202023%20report%20from%20the,47%25%20of%20all%20employed%20individuals

Business Wire. A bright future for women in construction: Satisfaction, employment, gender equality all make significant strides in 2021. https://www.businesswire.com/news/home/20220310005950/en/A-Bright-Future-for-Women-in-Construction-Satisfaction-Employment-Gender-Equality-all-Make-Significant-Strides-in-2021

Catalyst. (2019a). *Why diversity and inclusion matter: Quick take.* https://www.catalyst.org/research/why-diversity-and-inclusion-matter/

Catalyst. (2019b). *Quick take: Women in construction.* https://www.catalyst.org/research/women-in-construction/

Catalyst. (2021). *Quick take: Women in construction and science, technology, engineering, and mathematics (STEM)*. Catalyst. https:// www.catalyst.org/research/women-in-construction-and-science-technology-engineering-and-mathematics-stem/

Catalyst. (2022). *Quick take: Women in construction*. Catalyst. https://www. catalyst.org/research/women-in-construction/

CLT Recruiters. Paving the way: How women are easing the labor shortage and redefining the industry. https://www.cltrecruiters.com/blog/paving-the-way-how-women-are-easing-the-labor-shortage-and-redefining-the-industry

Deltek. (2023, March). https://deltek.com/en/blog/empowering-women-in-construction

Eskridge, R., & Carini, J. (2017). Breaking ground: Women in construction trades. *Labor Studies Journal*, *42*(3), 221–240.

Industry for Women. https://www.ncarb.org/blog/redefining-building-industry-women

International Monetary Fund. (2012). *Empowering women is smart economics*. https://www.imf.org/external/pubs/ft/fandd/2012/03/revenga. htm

Karen, M. K. (2021). https://www.woodworkingnetwork.com/news/ woodworking-industry-news/women-manufacturing-construction-see-numbers-rise

Kimmel, R. M., & Milner, L. (2020). Diversity and inclusion in the construction industry: An overview. *Journal of Construction Engineering and Management*, *146*(8), 04020089.

McKinsey & Company. (2018). *Delivering through diversity*. https://www. mckinsey.com/business-functions/organization/our-insights/delivering-through-diversity

McKinsey & Company. (2020). *Diversity wins: How inclusion matters*. McKinsey & Company. https://www.mckinsey.com/business-functions/ organization/our-insights/diversity-wins-how-inclusion-matters

National Association of Women in Construction (NAWIC). (n.d.). https:// www.nawic.org/

National Association of Women in Construction (NAWIC). (2021). *Diversity & inclusion: Why it matters in construction.* https://www.nawic. org/nawic/default.asp

National Association of Women in Construction (NAWIC). (2023). *Women in construction: State of the industry report.* NAWIC.

National Council of Architectural Registration Boards (NCARB). Redefining the building industry for women. https://www.ncarb.org/blog/redefining-building-industry-women

Opportunity International. (2017, March). Empowered women make a difference and change the world. https://opportunity.org/news/blog/2017/03/empowered-women-change-the-world

Padavic, I., Ely, R., & Reid, E. (2020). Explaining the persistence of gender inequality: The work–family narrative as a social defense against the 24/7 work culture. *Administrative Science Quarterly, 65*(1), 61–111.

Powell, A., & Sang, K. (2013). Equality, diversity, and inclusion in the construction industry. *Construction Management & Economics, 31*(8), 795–801.

Safer Me. Women in construction – Building the future. https://www.safer. me/blog/women-in-construction-building-the-future/

Sang, K., & Powell, A. (2012). Gender inequality in the construction industry: Lessons from Pierre Bourdieu. In C. Greed (Ed.), *Making better places: Gender, diversity and inclusion* (pp. 174–188). British Library.

Society of Women Engineers (SWE). (2022). https://www.swe.org/

Tippett, R. (2018). Harassment architect: The role of sexual harassment in shaping women's experience in construction. *Australasian Journal of Construction Economics and Building, 18*(2), 24.

Turner, K., & Edgell, L. (2018). *Women in construction: Navigating a male-dominated industry.* Routledge.

United Nations. (2015). Transforming our world: The 2030 agenda for sustainable development. https://sdgs.un.org/goals/gender-equality

United Nations Development Programme. (2023). *Breaking ground: Empowering women in the construction industry.* UNDP.

United Nations Educational, Scientific and Cultural Organization
(UNESCO). (2020). Cracking the code: Girls' and women's education in
STEM. https://en.unesco.org/news/cracking-code-girls-and-womens-
education-stem

University of Oregon. (2024, January 17). *Empowering women in the
workforce worldwide.* https://research.uoregon.edu/about/
announcements/empowering-women-workforce-worldwide

U.S. Bureau of Labor Statistics. (2022). *Construction and extraction
occupations.* https://www.bls.gov/ooh/construction-and-extraction/home.
htm

Women in Construction UK. (2023). *Women in construction: The case for
change.* Women in Construction.

Women in construction: The state of the industry in 2023. BigRentz.

World Bank. (2023, February 21). *Empowering women to shape the future
of jobs.* https://live.worldbank.org/en/event/2023/empowering-women-
shape-future-jobs

World Economic Forum. (2020). *Global gender gap report 2020.* https://
www.weforum.org/reports/gender-gap-2020

Worrall, L., Harris, K., Thomas, A., McDermott, P., & Conway, C. (2010).
Barriers to women in the UK construction industry. *Engineering,
Construction, and Architectural Management.* https://doi.org/10.1108/
09699981011038060

4

CULTURE AND ENVIRONMENT OF THE CONSTRUCTION INDUSTRY

ABSTRACT

Creating our built environment is largely the responsibility of the dynamic and complex construction industry. This business is made up of a wide range of people who work together to construct buildings and infrastructure projects, from contractors and labourers to architects and engineers. Aside from its observable results, the construction sector has a particular culture and atmosphere that are formed by a special fusion of history, creativity and teamwork. The culture and environment in which the construction industry functions are the main topics of this section of the book.

Keywords: Culture; construction; environment; industry; participation; women

1. ENVIRONMENT OF THE CONSTRUCTION INDUSTRY

The construction industry (CI) operates under a complicated environment that includes a wide array of laws, rules, codes, policies and guidelines at the international, national and local levels. In numerous industrialised nations, the regulatory framework is comprehensive, encompassing various domains such as building and subdivision control, workplace health and safety, environmental protection and financial rules. Nevertheless, in developing nations, the construction regulatory framework is still in the process of being established and is divided into various parts, which makes it challenging to adhere to the regulations. The environmental issues encountered in the building industry pertain to the degree of execution and enforcement of rules rather than their creation. Essential components of the construction regulatory framework are building rules and standards, contracting regulations, planning laws, subdivision restrictions and zoning ordinances. Building codes prescribe the minimal criteria and benchmarks to secure building, whereas planning laws govern the use of land. Contracting guidelines establish a framework for collaboration among construction parties. Although developing countries have established certain standards, the effective application and enforcement of these policies, particularly at the local level where most building operations occur, nevertheless pose significant challenges. The construction sector is also impacted by a deficient institutional framework for the development, coordination and oversight of regulatory compliance. The construction business is characterised by a widespread culture that involves conflicting stakeholder agendas and relationships, as well as low regard for people and the environment. The construction sector is characterised by a performance-driven culture that prioritises short-term gains over long-term sustainability. In recent decades, the majority of companies have experienced significant changes and have integrated advancements in both products and processes as fundamental components of their operations. The engineering and construction industry has failed to keep up with technology advancements that may enhance production and productivity. Consequently, labour productivity has also remained stagnant. This situation can be attributed to various internal and external challenges. These challenges encompass the industry's persistent fragmentation, difficulties in recruiting a skilled workforce, insufficient connections with contractors and suppliers and inadequate knowledge transfer between projects. To achieve greater effectiveness and efficiency in the sector, it is necessary to implement digitalisation, adopt new building techniques, and embrace innovations such as prefabrication.

Digitalisation and innovations in the building industry can enhance sustainability. In recent times, certain novel ideas implemented in the prefabrication industry have shown their capacity to enhance the sustainability of construction projects and procedures. The advancements brought about by the Fourth Industrial Revolution facilitated the shift of prefabrication towards Industry 4.0. The fourth industrial revolution 4.0 or Industry 4.0 has introduced digital technologies, sensor systems, intelligent machines, and smart materials to the construction industry where Building Information Modelling (BIM) has become the central repository for collating digital information about a project. The industry consumes vast quantities of energy and produces substantial volumes of garbage. Given its significant environmental impact and substantial waste output, the construction industry is seen as a crucial sector that requires thorough investigation in the pursuit of sustainability. The prioritisation of immediate cost and time goals takes precedence over concerns for the environment, quality, and worker well-being. These cultural problems infiltrate the construction process in opposition to sustainable standards.

1.1 Culture of the Construction Industry

A significant number of developing nations' construction industries are still influenced by the traditional sociocultural practices and belief systems that have been in place for a long time (Lopez, 2023). Because these traditions devalue the role that women play and the general intelligence that they possess, the construction industry is commonly perceived as a male-dominated field. The discriminatory recruitment and employment practices, low respect for women, sexism, intimidation and overall macho culture that are prevalent in construction companies are all factors that contribute to the manifestation of male gender superiority (Wang, 2021). It is through current employees and managerial staff who were socialized under these traditions that the cultural mindset that is detrimental to women can permeate construction organisations.

In general, the construction business is not fit for females because of the qualities that make it tough and improper for them to work. It is commonly believed that women do not possess the kind of physical strength and capacity to resist tough conditions that are required for construction management positions. Many labour roles in the craft industry, such as excavation, which required a significant amount of strength, were considered to be male-dominated (Brown & Ralph, 1996). When taken as a whole, the hardworking conditions in the construction sector, in conjunction with the deeply ingrained prejudices about feminine frailty, dissuade women from entering the industry. This perspective is heightened by the stresses that are present on the construction site, while the poor degree of comfort that is present amplifies it.

2. LEVEL OF WOMEN'S PARTICIPATION IN THE CONSTRUCTION INDUSTRY

Based on empirical data acquired from construction companies, it was found that women made up an average of only 16.3% of the entire workforce across a variety of occupational categories (Garcia, 2021). There were just 10% of women who were craftspeople, which is the lowest ranking. When it comes to skilled positions, women excelled in administrative staff positions, accounting for 37.5% of the total. On the other hand, out of the 16.3% of women who were employed, only 10% of them were holding management positions (Garcia, 2021). The proportion of female professionals to male professionals in the construction industry was found to be less than one to four in other developing countries such as Colombia and Latin America, according to research statistics (Martinez, 2020). In comparison to the number of males working in the construction business, the percentage of women who are employed in the industry continues to be disproportionately low (Garcia, 2021). According to this, the preference for male labour is likely to continue to be a general tendency. In addition, the disparity in mean employment levels demonstrates that women are underrepresented in contrast to their male counterparts (Garcia, 2021).

3. EMPLOYMENT STATUS OF FEMALES IN THE CONSTRUCTION INDUSTRY

Over time, women's job situation in the construction business has improved gradually but noticeably (Smith, 2022a, 2022b, 2022c, 2022d, 2022e). Because construction has always been seen as a physically hard and male-oriented job, women have had less possibilities in it (Johnson, 2021a, 2021b, 2021c, 2021d). But more women are pursuing jobs in construction as society views change and knowledge of gender equality rises, shattering pre-conceptions and tearing down barriers (Smith, 2022a, 2022b, 2022c, 2022d, 2022e). The growing presence of women in a variety of professions throughout the construction industry is a noteworthy feature of their employment status (Johnson, 2021a, 2021b, 2021c, 2021d). Although historically concentrated in support and administrative roles, women's representation in traditionally male-dominated fields like project management, engineering, architecture, and skilled trades like carpentry, plumbing, and electrical work has been steadily increasing (Smith, 2022a, 2022b, 2022c, 2022d, 2022e). In addition to exhibiting more gender equality, this role variety broadens the talent pool in the field (Johnson, 2021a, 2021b, 2021c, 2021d).

The building and construction industry is consistently ranked among the most important economic sectors in some countries. Nevertheless, women are grossly underrepresented in the construction industry, with figures indicating that only 10% of the workforce in this sector is comprised of women on average. The percentage of women employed in the construction industry in

Nigeria was 16.3%, according to a poll. This figure is significantly lower than the percentage of women employed in other industries. In a similar vein, women make up approximately half of the total workforce in the Europe, however, only 10% of the construction workforce is comprised of women. Even in sophisticated countries like the United Kingdom, where opportunities and regulations for women are significantly more progressive, and women continue to represent a disproportionately small percentage of the population. Also, the types of work that women mostly perform in the construction industry are often less technical than those performed by males. It was found that the majority of women working in the construction industry are employed in administrative, secretarial, or support roles, while only a small percentage are working in trades or professional positions within the construction industry. For instance, in Nigeria, 50% of the women who were employed were working in manual labour, while 37.5% were employed in administrative positions. Craftswomen made up only 2.5% of the total population. This serves as an example of the horizontal segregation that occurs in the world, where women make up the majority of "female-typed" types of roles. In addition, gender segregation is reflected in the types of jobs that female employees hold, with the majority of them being administrative positions responsibilities. The majority of the women were engaged as workers, and they were responsible for carrying construction materials to the construction site. Within the administrative sector, around 37.5% held positions such as accounting and project documentation. Only a meagre 10% of men and 2.5% of women were employed in professional roles such as site supervision and craft trades, respectively. Several additional studies have revealed underrepresentation that is comparable to this one. For example, research conducted by Gurjao (2008) so far has discovered that the percentage of women working in the construction business in Australia was 11% and 10%, respectively. Women made up of only 7% of the pool of skilled workers in the construction industry in Turkey (Arslan & Kivrak, 2004).

Generally, the following are the elements that make up work roles in the construction industry:

> *Functions related to administration and clergy: It is estimated that a sizeable proportion of women who are employed in the CI are employed in administrative and clerical job positions. According to research conducted, about fifty to sixty percent of women who*

are engaged in the business are hired for secretarial, administrative,
and support service positions (Fielden et al., 2000). Typing, filing,
record keeping, bookkeeping, and other similar responsibilities are
included in these roles.

Women also make up a significant fraction of the workforce in construction, particularly in positions that require manual labour. Research conducted by Adeyemi et al. (2006) and Fielden et al. (2000) indicates that approximately 50–66% of female labourers are employed on construction sites, where they undertake activities such as hauling supplies and mixing concrete, among other things. The number of women who hold management positions in construction companies is quite low. Only a small percentage of men hold these jobs. A research conducted shows the percentage of women who hold management positions is somewhere between 6% and 10% (Fielden et al., 2000; Greed, 2000). The vast majority of these women are not employed in positions that are directly related to site-based technical or operations management; rather, they are involved in fields such as administration, human resources, health and safety respectively.

Professional and technical positions: In the construction industry, very few women are employed in professional or technical positions such as project management, estimating, design, planning, supervision and other similar positions or responsibilities. According to the statistics, professionals and technicians in the construction industry employ fewer than 5% of women (Fielden et al., 2000). Furthermore, when the employment categories are taken into consideration, this segmentation becomes even more apparent. Studies indicate that there were 71 male staff working in management and supervision, while there were only 18 female workers. This translates to a percentage of 79.7% for male personnel and 16.3% for female personnel. In terms of clerical personnel, 434 males made up 62% of the entire clerical workforce, while there were 267 females who made up 38% of the total. The gender gap was observed more clearly in occupations related to craft trades, where only 18 out of 999 crafts persons were female, which is equivalent to 1.8% of the total. These results are consistent with trends observed on a global scale. Only nine percent of the workforce in the construction business in the United Kingdom is comprised of women even though this does not imply that women are incapable of doing things, it does suggest that women are offered fewer possibilities for employment in comparison to their male counterparts. Findings of a research conducted highlights that around 6% of skilled construction occupations in Europe were held by women. Undoubtedly, changing attitudes, aggressive actions and growing appreciation of the value of diversity have all contributed to the improvement of women's employment status in the construction industry in recent years. In the industry, women are contributing significantly to a variety of professions by bringing new ideas, abilities and inventiveness to the table. But attaining true gender equality in the construction industry will need ongoing efforts to get beyond enduring obstacles and establish a setting that supports the success and well-being of every person, regardless of gender. The construction sector can fully use the potential of its diverse workforce and propel sustainable growth and innovation in the years to come by cultivating an inclusive culture, advocating for equal opportunity and removing structural hurdles.

3.1 Barriers to Women Employment in the Construction Industry

The construction sector, which is renowned for its resilience and crucial role in forming the physical environment, has long been associated with a workforce that is predominately male (Johnson, 2021a, 2021b, 2021c, 2021d). Women still encounter substantial obstacles to entry and promotion in the construction business, despite progress made in other areas towards gender equality (Smith, 2022a, 2022b, 2022c, 2022d, 2022e). These obstacles, which have their roots in institutional procedures, workplace cultures and social conventions, prevent women from fully participating in the sector and reduce its potential for diversity and innovation (Johnson, 2021a, 2021b, 2021c, 2021d). Several constraints have been there for women to enter the construction sector due to several variables that militate against their participation. According to studies, the "macho" culture of the sector is a significant obstacle (Smith, 2022a, 2022b, 2022c, 2022d, 2022e). This culture is characterised by elements such as hostility and conflict, as well as characteristics that women are considered to be incapable of managing (Johnson, 2021a, 2021b, 2021c, 2021d). Because of the bad image that has been established as a result of the poor portrayal of construction labour, women are less likely to imagine themselves working in the construction industry (Smith, 2022a, 2022b, 2022c, 2022d, 2022e). The lack of role models to encourage younger women, prejudice in recruiting and preferential treatment given to men in recruitment, promotion and training opportunities are some of the additional obstacles that prevent women from achieving their full potential in the construction Industry. Several factors are considered to be inhibitive, including working conditions that require physical exertion of strength for jobs such as lifting, climbing and working long hours under the sun (Smith, 2022a, 2022b, 2022c, 2022d, 2022e). Maintaining a career in construction can be difficult for several reasons, including the fact that family obligations require making sacrifices between one's profession and the care of children and family (Johnson, 2021a, 2021b, 2021c, 2021d). Women's confidence in their ability to perform specific tasks is further undermined by the prevalence of stereotypical views regarding their physical and mental capacities. The competitiveness that exists within the industry is a setback because it encourages unhealthy competition and cliques that are damaging to the advancement of women. In order to overcome the major obstacles preventing women from obtaining employment in the construction sector, industry players must work together. By utilising a wide pool of people and viewpoints, breaking down these obstacles would not only help achieve gender equality but also help the sector reach its full potential. In order to create settings where women may flourish and make important contributions to the construction sector, initiatives that attempt to dispel structural biases, promote inclusive workplace cultures and challenge preconceptions are essential. The construction sector can set itself up for long-term success, innovation and sustainable growth by promoting an environment of equality, respect and opportunity (Johnson, 2021a, 2021b, 2021c, 2021d).

3.2 Cultural Barriers to Entry and Retention in the Industry

One possible explanation for the existence of such limitations is the socio-cultural environment that is typical of emerging civilisations such as Nigeria (Johnson, 2021a, 2021b, 2021c, 2021d). Traditional beliefs, attitudes, and conventions have created a set of circumstances in which female capabilities are undermined and disadvantageous from the time they are an infant. Construction methods are deeply rooted in male domains and are affected by cultural and historical traditions. It is because of these traditions that women are not allowed to pursue employment in the construction industry. The culture of the construction business is similarly characterised by male domination overall. Also, construction sites are depicted as demanding and hostile environments that are characterised by "macho" behaviours such as taking risks, maintaining physical endurance and engaging in verbal conflict. A culture that is controlled by men contributes to the perpetuation of gender stereotypes that exclude women because they are unable to meet the expectations of the culture. (As a result of this, women internalise these pictures and make the decision that a job in construction is not a viable option for them (Smith, 2022a, 2022b, 2022c, 2022d, 2022e)).

3.3 Policies and Formulations Done to Improve Women Status

Several policies and methods, both on a global and national scale, have been developed in order to solve the numerous obstacles that have been encountered. Conventions that have been approved on a global scale have declared that the right to gender equality is a fundamental human opportunity. The Convention on the Elimination of All Forms of Discrimination against Women (CEDAW) is one example of such a convention (Smith, 2022a, 2022b, 2022c, 2022d, 2022e). Both bodies and agreements have voiced their disapproval of the existing institutional imbalances. With the passage of laws and the implementation of various programmes of action, affirmative actions have been further promoted. In Nigeria, there is legislation that prohibits discrimination against individuals on the basis of their gender in public offices. This legislation is at the national level. There are a number of professional organisations that have also incorporated women into their policy recommendations and strategy goals. Plans for equality have been produced by public organisations in crystal clear detail. Generally, these coordinated efforts are in accordance with the worldwide mission to advance the empowerment of women in the construction industry in order to achieve the goals of sustainable development. Despite the actions of legislative bodies, the participation of women continues to lag behind. It may be deduced from this that attitudes that go beyond positive laws continue to be issues that function as obstacles (Smith, 2022a, 2022b, 2022c, 2022d, 2022e). There is still a need for a cultural revolution that is centred on the industry, as well as the mainstreaming of female characteristics through open enlightenment over an extended period of time. It is imperative that policies go beyond regulation in order to target the mindset of society, while simultaneously enabling flexible working arrangements and reward systems in order to keep women in the construction industry. There should be action taken by the government to validate implementation with monitoring in order to foster women participation in the construction industry (Johnson, 2021a, 2021b, 2021c, 2021d).

3.4 Construction Company Policies and Practices

Even though there is legislation that makes discrimination illegal, women still face obstacles when trying to enter organisations and advance their careers. The industry's laissez-faire human resource strategies and its lack of family-friendly rules might make the work-life conflict that women experience even more difficult to manage. Low levels of organizational commitment to equality for both men and women are characterised by the absence of gender audits and action plans, as well as a lack of statistical monitoring and ambiguity regarding the role of human resources. Women are marginalised when there is bias in the recruiting process, or when priority is given to applicants who display typical masculine characteristics. Women receive lower scores in performance reviews, which contributes to the perpetuation of gender bias. The absence of mentoring prevents women from receiving career coaching. Women who earn less than men are more likely to be dissatisfied with their jobs and to have less devotion to their work.

3.5 Strategies to Improve Female Participation in Construction

Inadequate representation of women in the construction industry necessitates the implementation of multi-pronged strategies in order to both attract a greater number of women to the industry and keep them (Smith & Johnson, 2021a, 2021b, 2021c, 2021d). At the policy, workplace and societal levels, the strategies need to make an all-encompassing effort to overcome the obstacles and these comprise of:

• Gender mainstreaming initiatives targeting the construction policy to align with inclusivity are included in this category. These initiatives are implemented at the government and policy level.

• The allocation of financial resources for programmes and initiatives that aim to alter attitudes and behaviours with regard to the roles that women play in the construction industry.

• Frameworks for regulatory oversight that ensure compliance monitoring and non-discriminatory activities are monitored to ensure females are recruited in the industry.

At the level of the organisation or workplace:

(1) Integrating a culture of diversity by implementing gender-sensitive policies, training and fair employment practices (Smith, 2022a, 2022b, 2022c, 2022d, 2022e). The implementation of effective work-life balance measures, such as flexible work arrangements, support for childcare and policies on parental leave.

(2) Programmes where women can network with one another and receive mentoring.

- Keeping an eye out for any instances of discrimination through equal pay and promotion procedures.

- In order to bring about cultural change at the social level, the following should be done:

- Use media outreach and school programmes to challenge negative stereotyped ideas. The promotion of success stories and role models in order to encourage women involvement and participation in the industry.

- Support networks for shared experience and peer motivation for women

Creating a culture transformation through a comprehensive, multi-front strategy should be accomplished by the adoption of strategies that incorporate both hard law techniques and soft law voluntary measures. By addressing the difficulties in a holistic manner at the policy, workplace and societal levels, the construction industry has a better opportunity of creating a climate that is conducive to women achieving a balance in their identities in the construction industry on equal terms with men (Smith, 2022a, 2022b, 2022c, 2022d, 2022e).

4. QUALITIES AND ABILITIES ASSOCIATED WITH WOMEN

4.1 Potential Qualities and Abilities of the Women in the Construction Industry

According to the findings of research, there are a number of skills and characteristics that women possess that would make it possible for them to achieve success in the construction occupation. A few examples of them are their ability to communicate effectively, tendency to work well with others, ability to multitask, precision, and focus on safety. Generally, women are more likely to have stronger communication abilities than men. These skills include active listening, verbal and non-verbal expression, the ability to recognise the viewpoints of others and the ability to facilitate working together. There have been a number of studies that have demonstrated that women are better able to collect and communicate information through verbal and non-verbal channels. A significant amount of coordination and collaborative effort from a wide variety of stakeholders is required for construction activity. These are a few of the most important advantages that women contribute to construction roles.

Women exhibit greater tendencies towards teamwork and collaboration than those who are male. They engage in collaborative efforts, aim to reach an agreement and establish networks of mutual support. These types of activities help the development of relationships, the settlement of conflicts and the collective problem-solving that is essential in multi-party construction projects. Men have a tendency to engage in behaviours that are more individualistic and competitive as compared to women. Also, research has revealed that women are more capable of combining many tasks than men are. In the dynamic construction sector, which is characterised by uncertainties, time demands and changing priorities, the capacity to simultaneously manage a variety of duties is essential. Women also exhibit a better level of precision for their actions. Precision means paying attention to details, maintaining order and being accurate. The outcomes of construction projects are strongly dependent on meticulous documentation, planning and craftsmanship.

Other research found that women have a higher level of safety orientation compared to men. They are less likely to ignore potential dangers and waste time and resources. There are a number of beneficial traits that are associated with employing women the construction sector, including a focus on health and safety regulations as well as jobsite risks. These characteristics, whether they are natively possessed or acquired through time and experience, have the ability to qualify and enable women to achieve success as competent professionals in the construction industry (Smith & Johnson, 2021a, 2021b, 2021c, 2021d).

4.2 Challenges Militating Against Women's Participation in the Construction Industry Amidst Their Potentials

On the other hand, a number of societal pressures also contribute to the development of characteristics among women that create difficulties in the building sector. According to research, socialisation tactics teach girls obedience and compliance at an early age, and they also decrease the likelihood that they will take risks. Also, women may have a tough time fitting into the dominant culture of the construction workplace, which is characterised by aggressiveness, risk-taking and aggressive self-promotion. According to research, the media and traditional gender role expectations frequently portray construction as a role that is traditionally associated with men and is not appropriate for women. A child's job goals are influenced by this from an early age. Women who pursue careers that are not traditionally associated with women, such as teaching and nursing, are more likely to attract pleasure and rapport from their families and communities as compared to their counterparts who opt for jobs dominated by men. Also, girls are discouraged from exploring non-traditional career possibilities such as construction due to influence from their peers, discouragement from their parents and a lack of career counselling opportunities. Lastly, women continue to undertake the majority of domestic tasks, including those related to household chores and childcare, even when they are employed. Construction is characterised by lengthy work hours, inflexible scheduling and unsocial hours, all of which make it difficult to maintain a healthy balance between one's professional and personal life. The difficulties that women face in the sector make it difficult for them to remain employed and advance their careers in the industry.

4.3 Policies Implemented and Yet to Be Implemented to Promote Women's Participation in the Construction Industry

It is necessary to strengthen policies that address the existing challenges to effectively utilise the potential of women in the construction industry. Several industrialised countries have implemented flexible work programmes, improved gender pay equity regulations and industry efforts that are geared towards women (Smith, 2022a, 2022b, 2022c, 2022d, 2022e). It has been ascertained that governments and construction authorities encourage a better work-life balance, opportunities for women to network and awareness of non-traditional career paths beginning at a younger age. A culture that is more visible and caters to women can be established through the implementation of family-friendly infrastructure, which goes beyond basic diversity policies. On the other hand, continual underrepresentation indicates that there is room for more effective intervention. It is possible to reduce discrimination by passing pay legislation and enforcing it stringently. The promotion of paid maternity leave and excellent part-time and job-share roles with matching benefits opens up new choices for managing the demands of a career and a family. Research has shown that educational outreach that dispels gender misconceptions and highlights success stories can encourage interest and confidence in non-traditional choices at a young age (Smith, 2022a, 2022b, 2022c, 2022d, 2022e). Women's participation can also be increased through aggressively recruiting and sponsoring with a backbone of mentoring and apprenticeship programmes. Also, employers should make sure that their workplaces are places where women are treated with respect and worth, and where they are evaluated based on their true level of competence, independent of their gender.

A fair playing field is normalised when policies against harassment, flexible working hours and the possibility to work remotely are in place (Johnson, 2021a, 2021b, 2021c, 2021d). It is also possible to reduce the influence of implicit prejudice by ensuring diversity on review committees and interview panels. The disparity in representation will inevitably continue to exist if purposeful reforms are not implemented to address the structural obstacles that restrict the presence and success of women. Only via interventions that take place on multiple levels is it possible to fully realize the capabilities of women and to achieve true diversity and inclusion in the construction industry (Johnson, 2021a, 2021b, 2021c, 2021d).

5. WOMEN DISCRIMINATION

5.1 Discrimination of Women in the Construction Industry

According to the International Labour Organisation, the construction industry has traditionally been considered a male-dominated sector with deeply ingrained ideas of masculinity. Much research has found that the construction industry is rife with instances of discrimination and inequality towards women. This has been confirmed by the existing body of literature, in their study, Michel and Clegg underlined the fact that the construction industry is often structured in a manner that is unattractive to women, preventing them from gaining access to positions of authority and responsibility. According to a study that was carried out by Özbay, it was discovered that women encounter uneven treatment in the workplace as a result of their interactions with customers, colleagues and bosses. They frequently do not have access to possibilities for professional growth and training. Women in the construction sector have the perception that they are not being taken seriously by their professional peers. According to research, they are subjected to blatant acts of hostility from their coworkers and clients, who make derogatory comments about their capabilities and performances while they are on the job. There are situations in which women have the impression that they are being given menial tasks that are not commensurate with their skills. The perspectives and viewpoints of women are frequently disregarded or ignored during meetings. Women are unable to access chances within the construction industry because of discrimination that occurs during the initial training phase of the recruitment process. Also, job advertisements for construction tasks are typically written in a gendered manner, emphasising physical strength and endurance as prerequisites. This creates barriers for female applicants who are interested in applying for these positions. It has also been discovered that interviewers and managers of human resources have preconceived notions about the capabilities of women. One of the perceptions that exist is the idea that labour in the construction industry demands a level of physical strength that women do not possess.

5.2 The Influence That Discrimination Has on the Inclusion of Women in the Construction Industry

Discriminatory behaviours and attitudes within the industry hurt how women advance their careers and remain employed within the sector (Johnson, 2021a, 2021b, 2021c, 2021d). Research has found that women who experience feelings of being undervalued, marginalised and a lack of support are more likely to experience stress, which in turn leads to a drop in their dedication and performance at work. Also, women are compelled to completely give up their employment in the construction industry as a result of unpleasant encounters. It has been demonstrated through research that prejudice prevents women from making full use of their skills and talents, which in turn limits the potential contribution that women could make to the aims of an organisation. In many cases, these lead to low levels of self-esteem and confidence, which in turn has an effect on women's leadership qualities and their aspirations for their careers (Smith, 2022a, 2022b, 2022c, 2022d, 2022e). It has been discovered that discrimination induces a "chilly climate" that promotes the invisibility and quiet attitude of women within teams that are controlled by men. It erects obstacles that prevent women from being accepted, respected, and influential, particularly in settings where decisions are made. The beliefs and viewpoints that they hold are frequently disregarded or minimised. This prevents organisations from benefiting from the variety of perspectives and methods of problem-solving that women contributes (Smith, 2022a, 2022b, 2022c, 2022d, 2022e).

5.3 Policies to Reduce Discrimination

On a global scale, some rules and measures have been implemented to combat discrimination and encourage the inclusion of women in the buildings and construction industry. The Employment Equity Act (EEA No. 55 of 1998), the Broad-Based Black Economic Empowerment Act (BBBEE Act No. 53 of

2003), the Skills Development Act (SDA No. 97 of 1998), the Skills Development Levies Act (SDLA No. 9 of 1999), the National Skills Development Strategy (NSDSI 2005–2010) and the Affirmative Procurement and Implementation Strategy developed in 2007 were all pieces of legislation that were enacted at the national level in South Africa.

"Women in Construction" and "Women Empowerment Framework" are two examples of the efforts that the government of South Africa has undertaken. Specifically, these initiatives attempted to encourage women to engage in entrepreneurial activity by means of procurement, empowerment courses, and advocacy. Skinner and Maude produced a set of guidelines with the intention of addressing the issue of change in the business by ensuring that women are included in decision-making, receiving training and having access to economic possibilities.

Convention No. 111 of the International Labour Organisation, which was adopted in 1958, encourages non-discrimination in the workplace. Equal compensation for equal effort is guaranteed by International Labour Organisation Convention No. 100 (1951). Other international instruments that are utilised include the United Nations Economic and Social Commission for Africa's Equal Participation Recommendation No. 9, the United Nations Convention on the Elimination of Discrimination Against Women and the Beijing Platform for Action, which were endorsed during the Fourth World Conference on Women in 1995 through the United Nations Women.

In order to encourage the participation of women in the construction industry, response measures have been put into place by both the private sector and the government. Studies have demonstrated that there is a limited impact on the retention and development of women inside construction businesses for women. As a result, there is a need for further actions to be taken in order to effectively address barriers against discrimination and to promote inclusivity and equality for women working in the construction business.

Despite opportunities from flexible work programmes, changing societal attitudes and some legal rudiments, structural barriers persist limiting advancement. Women remain underrepresented in construction executive roles due to leaky career pipelines and lack of access to strategic networks. Improving the representation of women in top positions requires addressing obstacles holistically through multi-pronged strategies targeting policy reform and cultural transformation.

5.4 Impact of Discrimination on Women's Absorption in the Industry

Discrimination leads to women facing additional barriers in advancing their careers in the construction industry (Brown, 2021a, 2021b, 2021c). Research shows that discriminatory experiences increase stress levels in women, negatively impacting their mental health and job commitment. Prolonged stress can manifest physically over the long-term as well if left unaddressed.

Discrimination is also found to undermine women's self-confidence in their abilities. Being subjected to unequal treatment and having their skills constantly questioned chips away at self-esteem. With reduced belief in their capabilities, women may hesitate pursuing new qualifications or roles that could aid career progression. The constant doubt and unfairness sowed by discrimination can become a self-fulfiling prophecy, limiting ambition and risk-taking.

Studies moreover link discrimination to growing dissatisfaction with organisations among affected women. Not feeling valued and constantly facing unfairness breeds resentments that translate to lowered dedication (Brown, 2021a, 2021b, 2021c). Women may then seek career changes, directly reducing the company's investment in their development. Indirectly, high turnover means the valuable qualities and perspectives women offer are also lost to the firm. These detrimental impacts ultimately serve to further entrench the underrepresentation discrimination itself as an initial cause.

It has been demonstrated through research that prejudice makes it more difficult for women to obtain equal chances and to advance their careers in construction companies (Brown, 2021a, 2021b, 2021c). Women's organisational engagement and job satisfaction levels are lowered as a result of discriminatory encounters, which ultimately leads to their departure from the industry. In addition, this contributes to the fact that they are underrepresented in the industry.

An investigation conducted by Fiedler in 2017 among tradeswomen in Canada indicated that they were subjected to high levels of stress as a result of unfair treatment, which affected both their mental and physical health. Negative experiences, such as antagonism from coworkers, can cause psychological distress, which in turn can increase the likelihood that affected women will leave their jobs. Due to the fact that it causes individuals to have low self-confidence regarding their ability to apply the abilities that they have learnt, discrimination may also prevent individuals from updating their qualifications.

The female talent pool is further reduced as a result of discrimination, which in turn reduces the industrial sector's overall productivity (Brown,

2021a, 2021b, 2021c). As a result, businesses lose the competitive advantage that comes from having a diverse set of abilities and points of view. According to research, the failure of businesses and the economy as a whole inhibits the use of human capital to its full potential.

In conclusion, discriminatory practices hinder the advancement of the sector by preventing women from making important career advancements and preventing them from having equal chances. The fact that it prevents prospective female students from contemplating employment in the construction industry is a significant obstacle. Generally, it contributes to the underutilisation of women's skills, which has a detrimental effect on the performance of businesses and the expansion of the economy.

In general, discrimination poses multidimensional challenges that extend beyond direct barriers like unequal opportunities. By increasing stress, undermining self-esteem and fostering dissatisfaction, discrimination often completes the push for women to withdraw from the industry they initially encountered barriers in. A truly inclusive structure requires conscious efforts to overcome all forms of discrimination for women to achieve equitable empowerment (Brown, 2021a, 2021b, 2021c).

6. WOMEN LEADERSHIP IN THE CONSTRUCTION INDUSTRY

6.1 Categories of Various Positions Held by Women in the Construction Industry

There is a wide range of employment available to women in the construction sector, ranging from those that are non-management to those that are in leadership positions (Smith, 2022a, 2022b, 2022c, 2022d, 2022e). The jobs of assistants, trainers and designers are examples of non-management positions. These positions are typically self-directed. Supervisory occupations often consist of a supporting function to middle management. Examples of supervisory roles include management consultants and project managers. Middle management positions include functions such as facilities managers, contract managers and senior quantity surveyors (Smith, 2022a, 2022b, 2022c, 2022d, 2022e). These individuals are primarily accountable for overseeing the entirety of the project processes and guiding project teams. Senior management responsibilities include company directors, company partners and project directors, and all of these roles frequently include making decisions that affect the entire organisation. In addition, women make up the majority of those working in the teaching profession because, historically speaking, it has been considered an appropriate occupation for women (Smith, 2022a, 2022b, 2022c, 2022d, 2022e). A wide variety of positions, from assistant lecturers to professors, are available to women working in the construction industry.

An examination of the many roles that women have held in the past and the present in comparison to those held by males; the figures from the past two decades demonstrate that there has been an increase in the number of women who hold managerial positions in a variety of different businesses. The fact remains, however, that they are underrepresented in the construction industry (Johnson, 2021a, 2021b, 2021c, 2021d).

An investigation into the construction industry in the United Kingdom conducted in the past revealed that just 6.3% of construction managers were female (Harrison, 2010). Women make up only 9.9% of construction workers in the United States in 2018. Recent research has revealed that about 9% of construction workers in the United States are female. These low levels have been maintained because early and mid-career women have been forced out of the workforce by masculine culture. According to the US Department of Labour, even though women make up more than half of undergraduate students and more than a quarter of nursing graduates, their presence in the engineering business remains largely consistent. There has been an increase in the number of women holding managerial roles across all sectors of the economy; nonetheless, women continue to be underrepresented in executive positions within the construction industry. In 2010, only 9% of construction managers were female, according to research that analysed data from the United States Bureau of Labour Statistics (Harrison, 2010). According to Harrison (2010) within the same time, women made up 6.3% of engineering managers. According to the findings of this study, only 3.9% of executive positions in engineering were held by women while these total responsibilities were being considered. Although there has been an increase in the number of women who have graduated from engineering and construction programmes over the past 24 years, women continue to be underrepresented in the construction sector and in executive positions within the construction business. It is difficult for the sector to convert the growing number of female candidate pools into long-term engagement and leadership inside the construction industry.

Comparison of the many roles that women have held in the past and in the present in comparison to those held by males; Attrition throughout all career stages contributes to consistent underrepresentation of women in the construction industry, despite the fact that the number of women entering the construction labour market is increasing. Research conducted since the 1970s has been tracking the difficulties that women face while entering blue-collar fields in terms of entry and retention. Women opt to leave the sector for a wide variety of personal and professional reasons. It has also been well established that there are barriers that prevent women from entering the industry.

When comparing women's positions in the past and the present, it is possible to see the impact that shifting gender boundaries has had over time. Although the percentage of females in management positions has increased from 6.3% in 1980 to 10.5% in 2018, construction executives continue to be less than 10%. Limited transformation is a reflection of structural impediments as opposed to individual barriers that were discussed earlier.

The "Leaky pipeline" hypothesis of women leaving the sector because they are unable to advance is supported by the fact that women are underrepresented across all levels of their careers. As a result of greater rates of women leaving the workforce, increases in enrolment do not transfer into increased workforce representation. As a result of a lack of representation in management, women are unable to advance in their careers (Smith, 2022a, 2022b, 2022c, 2022d, 2022e). Despite the fact that graduation rates have increased, women continue to be underrepresented in all construction jobs, from the workforce in the sector to executive roles. This suggests that individual hurdles as well as institutional concerns are the factors that discourage retention and promotion. The persistent lack of representation is evidence of a "leaky pipeline" that is removing qualified women from the workforce.

6.2 Untapped Potential of Women in the Construction Industry

According to recent research, women are more likely to be interested in jobs that are related to environmental protection. An investigation of the green industry's potential to recruit a greater number of women was conducted by comparing green construction enterprises relative to the overall sample. More women are being represented in environmentally conscious organisations. The performance of green enterprises was superior to that of non-green firms across all revenue segments, with women engineering executives achieving a percentage increase from 3.9%–6.2% (≤$250 million) to 3.3%–5.5% (>$1 billion). In addition to rises in most categories, the percentage of all-male businesses has decreased from 78.2% (non-green) to 65.8% (green), with the most notable increase being 11–20% (9.3–21.1%).

Women may be more likely to be interested in sustainability and the environment, which would also attract a bigger number of women. Green industries are brought closer to achieving bigger social impacts, which is considered a crucial driver for women who are looking for a purpose in their lives. There is a possibility that the impact of recruitment may be improved if leadership demonstrates a commitment to diversity and inclusion initiatives. Also, construction organisations that promote environmental stewardship have a higher percentage of women in executive positions in engineering than their non-green counterparts, despite the fact that the differences are statistically insignificant. There is the possibility for benefits to be gained by aligning missions with causes that attract women.

7. MENTORSHIP IN THE CONSTRUCTION INDUSTRY

7.1 General Mentorship in the Construction Industry

Mentoring plays a key role in facilitating the transfer of knowledge in the construction industry given its project-based nature (Kram, 2018a, 2018b, 2018c, 2018d). Effective mentoring requires fostering trusting relationships between experienced practitioners and newcomers while supporting professional and personal growth over time. While literature emphasises mentoring's benefits, construction remains understudied regarding effective mentor characteristics for women. Identifying such characteristics is vital for empowering underrepresented women groups through targeted programming.

The construction sector is characterised by its project-based nature and transient organizational structures, which makes mentoring an essential component of workplace-based learning in the construction industry. Construction work is a complex process that requires teams to coordinate their efforts and impart their skills to one another. This process brings together a wide variety of professions and trades. The purpose of mentorship is to increase performance by transferring knowledge and abilities from more experienced workers to others who are just starting out in their careers (Kram, 2018a, 2018b, 2018c, 2018d).

Mentoring in the South African construction industry was conducted to facilitate the transfer of skills and develop future industry leaders. Accordingly to Kram, a mentor is defined as someone who acts as a role model for a mentee and provides direction to the mentee by assisting with both professional and personal development over time. Effective mentoring in the construction industry demands dedication, guidance and trust between the individuals involved, regardless of whose gender or ethnicity the parties are. Mentors need to undergo training to acquire the appropriate interpersonal skills to transmit knowledge to mentees and support their learning and career-planning abilities. Effective mentoring leads to the development of innovative ideas and growth, both of which are essential for the competitiveness of an organisation in the dynamic construction industry environments. The benefits of mentoring in the workplace include the key components of knowledge transfer and experiential learning (Kram, 2018a, 2018b, 2018c, 2018d). As an information-intensive industry, construction is strongly dependent on mentorship as a means of imparting knowledge and enhancing the skills of novices while they are on the job. Although the practice of construction is distinct from that of normal office professions, mentorship serves the same purpose of aiding professional advancement (Kram, 2018a, 2018b, 2018c, 2018d).

7.2 Comparison of the Mentoring Responsibilities of Men and Women

Significant research has been carried out on mentoring experiences between males and females in both educational and corporate settings. These studies have been conducted in both corporate and educational settings. According to the findings of pioneering research conducted by Kalbfleisch and Keyton (2018), female mentees reported receiving a greater amount of psychosocial support and career coaching from their female mentors than their male counterparts (Kalbfleisch & Keyton, 2018). Twenge (2020) suggests that contemporary perspectives show that the gender effect in mentoring may be diminishing over time as cultural barriers become less pronounced (Twenge, 2020). It been suggested in literature that contemporary perspectives show that the gender effect in mentoring may be diminishing over time as cultural barriers become less pronounced.

There are minimal or insignificant differences in the mentoring functions that are received based on the gender of the mentor or the protégé.

Yet another significant finding is that women mentees consistently report gaining less from mentoring than their male counterparts. This is a finding that continues to be significant. This may be the result of assumptions and social constructions of masculinity that prevent male mentors from providing female protégés with the career and psychological support they need to succeed in their careers. Female mentees may additionally require individualised skill development that focuses on boosting their self-confidence and developing tactics to combat prejudice. These are the kinds of skills that are best suited for mentoring by female mentors who have personal experience. It is also important to consider the mentoring style, with Eby, which indicated that an androgynous approach that combines the strengths of both masculine and feminine mentoring may be the most effective technique. Although it has been demonstrated that mentoring experiences are less dependent on gender as social norms shift, disparities continue to exist, necessitating individualised support for women who are being mentored (Eby, 2021). By mentoring other women and gradually eradicating stereotypes within their own companies and the construction industry as a whole, women professionals in the construction industry could play a leading role in the development of other women. In order to accomplish this, they must demonstrate a dedication to promoting the status of other women through personal initiatives in addition to organised programmes (Eby, 2021).

7.3 Mentorship in Improving Mentee Performance

Studies have shown that successful mentoring can improve performance, as well as organisational commitment, employee retention and career outcomes. These benefits have been highlighted in a number of different ways. On an individual level, mentoring can be beneficial in the construction industry for the development of skills such as professionalism, problem solving and decision-making abilities, as well as technical, interpersonal and conceptual talents. In the context of quality assurance project management, for example, this could mean honing abilities in areas such as cost management, variations value, claims processing, contractual negotiations and dispute resolution. The integration of classroom theory into practice, the acquisition of industry-specific knowledge, and the development of soft skills are all further aided by mentoring. The graduates' ability to transfer into construction pro-fessions more seamlessly is improved as a result of these combined factors.

With mentorship supervision, female graduates can negotiate professional trajectories to take up technical specializations in quantity surveying needing field experience such as estimating, construction evaluation, value engineering or project management. They might progressively seek opportunities to learn management skills through guided apprenticeships leading to supervisory and leadership positions over time. Those who go for an entrepreneurial option benefit from mentored skills in business management, financial planning, risk assessment and marketing that enable firm development and growth. Success stories emanating from highly mentored women motivate and inspire other women.

Through the guidance and support of a mentor, mentees can develop the self-assurance that they are capable of advancing professionally provided they are consistent in their efforts. According to research, the development of "agentic" skills that are beneficial for professional growth is fostered by mentor–mentee relationships that are positively characterised. A more effective work–life balance can be achieved through mentoring by providing helpful career advice and role modelling that demonstrates that it is possible to attain this balance. Effective mentoring provides mentees with the tools necessary to overcome gender-based obstacles with resilience and inventiveness. The ability to adopt leadership roles and guide themselves towards realizing their full potential is facilitated, regardless of the gender of the individuals involved. When this is the case, mentoring is an extremely important factor in maintaining and improving the performance of female construction professionals.

It is evident that female construction professionals do encountered obstacles, but they also demonstrated that they are capable of achieving success when they are provided with equal opportunities and assistance. These are some mentorship traits that promote mentee performance; Discovering a mentor who is supportive: An experienced female mentor is essential not only for professional advice but also for navigating one's professions and overcoming doubts as the only females on sites. Women mentorship helps mentees to overcome the specific hurdles that are associated with their gender in the workplace. The maintenance of personal and professional networks: Engaging in interactions with professional colleagues through associations assists mentees in advancing their careers through the acquisition of knowledge and opportunities. In addition, support group's help women cope with their experiences by fostering a sense of community so that they can share their stories with one another. The need to comply to society norms is a difficult challenge for women, but through mentorship, individuals express resilience in managing the expectations of their family, clients and colleagues. In spite of the challenges, they rely on establishing rapport, demonstrating their skills and concentrating on the quality of their work.

Mentorship plays an essential part in the growth of a construction professional as well as the instillation of coping methods to overcome obstacles that are based on gender inequality. In situations where female mentors are not accessible, it might be useful for devoted guys to fill the position of a mentor in a constructive manner. When the contextual dynamics are taken into consideration, it is possible that the sector will require a variety of mentoring methodologies. However, the provision of psychosocial support is essential to the development of self-assurance and resiliency. There was a consensus that networking through professional organisations was advantageous. A female engineer expressed gratitude for exchanges that broadened her social circle and provided her with additional opportunities. Nevertheless, difficulties continue to arise when lengthy working hours come into conflict with family life. Although women valued financial benefits, they placed a higher priority on work flexibility in order to achieve a better work–life balance. Mentoring was difficult to get, yet it proved effective in boosting self-belief for all of the respondents (Ragins & Cotton, 2021). To achieve overall success, it was necessary to have support in order to balance numerous life roles. Through mentoring, workplace practices and ongoing education, it concludes by identifying techniques that can be utilised to encourage women's admission into the construction industry as well as their retention in the field. The establishment of a sufficiently large number of female role models at each stage is the foundation upon which females can be absolved and retained in the construction industry.

BIBLIOGRAPHY

Adani, J., & Associates. (2015). Ghana construction industry report [online]. http://www.adaniafrica.com/ghana-construction-industry-report/. Accessed on 25 October 2023.

Adedeji, A. Y., Oloke, D. O., Aina, O. O., & Oyeyipo, O. I. (2016). Dwindling rate of women's.

Adeyemi, A. Y., Ojo, S. O., Aina, O. O., & Olanipekun, E. A. (2004). Construction process rationalization strategies or sustainable mass housing delivery in Nigeria. In *Proceedings of XXXII-IAHS world housing congress, 3–4th April, 2004*. Delft University.

Adeyemi, A. Y., Oladipo, F. A., & Adewunmi, E. D. (2006). The role of women in the Nigerian construction industry. *Construction Management & Economics*, 24(6), 559–566.

Afolabi, A., Aigbavboa, C. O., & Thwala, W. D. (2017). *Evaluating the effects of craft training on.*

Agapiou, A. (2002). Perceptions of gender roles and attitudes toward work among male and female operatives in the Scottish construction industry. *Construction Management & Economics*, 20(8), 697–705. https://doi.org/10.1080/0144619021000024989

Agrawal, P., & Rahman, Z. (2015). Women in construction: The emerging workforce. *International Journal of Construction Management*, *15*(4), 341–352.

Ajayi, S. O., Oyedele, L. O., Bilal, M., Akinade, O. O., Alaka, H. A., & Owolabi, H. A. (2020). Deep learning and boosted trees for injuries prediction in power infrastructure projects. *Applied Soft Computing*, *110*, 107587.

Allen, C. A. (1992). Career patterns and role balance among professional Australian women in the decade of the eighties. *Australian Journal of Psychology*, *44*(2), 65–74. https://doi.org/10.1080/00049539208260177

Allison, M., & Kaminsky, S. (2017). Women in engineering: The leaky pipeline. In Z. N. Razzak (Ed.), *Engineering education innovation* (pp. 177–193). IntechOpen.

Amaratunga, D., Haigh, R., Lee, A., Shanmugam, M., & Elvitigala, G. (2006). Construction industry and women: A review of the barriers. *Journal of Construction in Developing Countries*, *11*(2), 1–19.

Amaratunga, D., Haigh, R., Shanmugam, M., Elvitigalage, D., & De Blois, M. (2006a). Construction industry and women: A review of the barriers. In *Proceedings of the 3rd international conference of CIB W107-creating a sustainable construction industry in developing countries, South Africa November 2006* (pp. 326–338).

Amaratunga, D., Haigh, R., Shanmugam, M., Elvitigalage, D., & De'Blois, N. (2006b). Construction industry and women: A review of the barriers. In *3rd international conference of SCRI research* (pp. 326–338). Delft.

Arditi, D., & Balci, G. (2009). Managerial competencies of male and female construction managers. *Journal of Construction Engineering and Management*, *135*(11), 1275–1278.

Arslan, G., & Kivrak, S. (2004). Issues encountered by women professionals in the Turkish construction sector. *Women in Management Review*, *19*(8), 408–421. https://doi.org/10.1108/09649420410563630

Australian Government Department of Employment. (2016, September). Labour force detailed quarterly, Australia. Detailed Australian Labour Market Data. https://www.employment.gov.au/labour-force-detailed-quarterly-data

Australian Government Workplace Gender Equality Agency. (2016, November). Australia's gender equality scorecard- key results. https://www.wgea.gov.au/sites/default/files/GEN%20Nov%20Scores%20Chart_0.pdf

Bagilhole, B., Dainty, A., & Neale, R. (2000). A grounded theory of women's career under-achievement in large UK construction companies. *Construction Management & Economics, 18*(2), 239–250.

Bass, B. M., & Avolio, B. J. (1994). Shatter the glass ceiling: Women may make better managers. *Human Resource Management, 33*(2), 549–560.

Bass, B. M., Avolio, B. J., & Atwater, L. (1996). The transformational and transactional leadership of men and women. *Applied Psychology, 45*, 5–34.

Bell, B. S., & Kurland, N. B. (2018). The effects of feedback sign and trustworthiness on feedback seeking and use. *Academy of Management Journal, 39*(6), 1615–1638.

Bencsik, A., Horváth-Csikós, G., & Juhász, T. (2014). Y and Z generations at workplaces. *Journal of Competitiveness, 6*(3), 90–106.

Bennett, J., Davidson, M., & Gale, A. (1999). Women in construction: A comparative investigation into the expectations and experiences of female and male construction undergraduates and employees. *Women in Management Review, 14*(7), 273–291.

Bjorkly, S. (2006). *Psychological theories of aggression: Principles and application to practice.* Springer Science + Business Media, LLC.

Bothelo, E., Gibson, P., Izzeldin, M., Ibanez, A. M., Liang, J., Phung, K., & Stewart, T. (2018). How long does it take to reach the top? Do middle and senior managers agree? *International Journal of Human Resource Management.* https://doi.org/10.1080/09585192.2018.1476231

Boucher, X., & Canalda, P. (2016). Building ethics into artificial intelligence. *Philosophical Transactions of the Royal Society A, 376*(2133).

Bowen, P., Edwards, P., Lingard, H., & Cattell, K. (2014). Occupational stress and job demand, control and support factors among construction project consultants. *International Journal of Project Management, 32*(7), 1273–1284.

Brink, H., & Stobbe, L. (2009). Gender relations at Swedish construction sites – Looking through a structural perspective. In S. L. Rama (Ed.),

Construction industry development and gender issues (pp. 156–174). New India Publishing Agency.

Brown, A. (2021a). Equal pay and promotion procedures: Strategies for combating discrimination in the construction industry. *Workplace Equality Quarterly, 15*(4), 90–105.

Brown, A. (2021b). Prejudice and its impact on women's career advancement in construction companies: An empirical investigation. *Gender Equality in Construction Journal, 25*(1), 30–45.

Brown, A. (2021c). Discrimination and its effects on job satisfaction and organizational engagement among women in construction: A longitudinal study. *Construction Management Review, 15*(4), 110–125.

Brown, M., & Ralph, S. (1996). Barriers to women managers' advancement in education in Uganda. *International Journal of Educational Management, 10*(6), 18–23.

Cassar, V., & Cortis, R. (2005). Perceptions of and about women as managers: Investigating job involvement, self esteem and attitudes. *Women in Management Review, 20*(3), 149–164.

Chao, G. T., Walz, P. M., & Gardner, P. D. (2022). Formal and informal mentorships: A comparison on mentoring functions and contrast with non-mentored counterparts. *Personnel Psychology, 48*(3), 581–604.

Construction Industry Training Board (CITB). (2003). Construction skills forecast report 2003. http://www.citb.co.uk. Accessed on September 2004.

Cordoano, M., Hines, F., Stafford, K., Mejia, A., & Warwood, S. (2002). Gender, culture, and customer orientation: Tests of differences among Argentinean and US salespeople. *Journal of International Business Studies, 33*(4). https://doi.org/10.1057/palgrave.jibs.8491015

Cubillo, L., & Brown, M. (2003). Women into educational leadership and management: International differences? *Journal of Educational Administration, 41*(3), 278–329.

da Mota Pedersen, V., & Costa, A. (2018). Challenges for recruiting women as construction site managers in Angola and Mozambique. *Journal of Construction in Developing Countries, 23*(2), 73–83.

Dainty, A., Bagilhole, B., Kinman, G., & Wellens, J. (2004). Work–life balances in construction: Glimpses of women's experiences. *Engage*, *1*(4), 36–40.

Dainty, A. R. J., Bagilhole, B. M., & Neale, R. H. (2000). A grounded theory of women's career under-achievement in large UK construction companies. *Construction Management & Economics*, *18*(2), 239–250.

Dainty, A. R. J., Bagilhole, B. M., & Neale, R. H. (2001). A grounded theory of women's career underachievement in large UK construction companies. *Construction Management & Economics*, *19*(2002), 2–14.

Dainty, A., & Edwards, D. (2003). The "fibreglass ceiling" revisited: Women's careers in a male-dominated industry. *Women in Management Review*, *18*(6), 312–319.

Dainty, A. R. J., Neale, R. H., & Bagilhole, B. M. (1999). Women in construction: A comparative investigation into the expectations and experiences of female and male construction under graduates and employees. In *Engineering, construction and architectural management*. Emerald Publishing Limited.

Dainty, A., Neale, R., & Bagilhole, B. (2000). Comparison of male and female perceptions of gender relations in UK construction sector organizations. *Engineering Construction Architecture Management*, *7*(2), 75–81.

Davey, C. L., Davidson, M. J., & Gale, A. W. (1999). Gender, pay and productivity differentials in the New Zealand construction industry. *Construction Management & Economics*, *17*(6), 755–767.

Davidson, M. J., & Burke, R. J. (2000). *Women in management: Current research issues volume II*. Sage Publications.

De Groot, H., & Schuitema, G. (2007). How to improve the quality of deliberation in the ecological domain? An overview of 25 strategic suggestions. *Quality and Quantity*, *41*(1), 81–92.

Dean, C. (2006). *Creating socially inclusive workplaces*. Chartered Management Institute.

Dellibovi, S., Luzi, D., O'Connor, J., Ghislieri, C., & Corti, S. (2016). *How to enhance gender diversity in construction. A focus on European policies and practices*. Publications Office of the European Union.

Department of Education. (1999). *NCES digest of education statistics* (Vol. 1999). https://nces.ed.gov/programs/digest/d99/d99t186.asp

Department of Labour. (2006). *Women in the labour market 1995–2005.* Republic of South Africa.

Devnew, L., Dewar, N., Furlong, P., & Doucet, A. (2018). Can't live with 'em; can't live without 'em: Gendered segmentation in the construction industry and its impact on health and safety. *Construction Management & Economics*, *36*(5), 245–258. https://doi.org/10.1080/01446193.2017.1387437

Eby, L. T. (2021). Androgynous mentoring styles: A strategy for effective mentoring. *Mentoring Strategies Journal*, *25*(1), 30–45.

Eccles, J. S. (1987). Gender roles and women's achievement-related decisions. *Psychology of Women Quarterly*, *11*(2), 135–172.

Edelman, L. B., & Petterson, S. (1993). The symbolic uses of illegality: Constructions of legitimacy in pedestrian begging. *Law & Society Review*, *27*(4), 819–848.

Ely, R. J., & Padavic, I. (2007). A feminist analysis of organizational research on sex differences. *Academy of Management Review*, *32*(4), 1121–1143.

European Commission. (2003). *Women and the information society.* Publication office of the European Communities.

Fenn, P., & Gameson, R. (Eds.). (1992). Construction conflict: Management and resolution (pp. 416–427). F.N. Spon.

Fiedler, A. S., O'Brien, R., & Haynes, S. (2017). Roofing skills challenge: Removing barriers for women in the skilled trades. *Work*, *56*(2), 275–281.

Fielden, S. L., Davidson, M. J., Gale, A. W., & Davey, C. L. (2000). Women in construction: The untapped resource. *Construction Management & Economics*, *18*(1), 113–121.

Fielden, S. L., Davidson, M. J., Gale, A. W., & Davey, C. L. (2001). Women in construction: The untapped resource. Construction management and economics. *Construction Management & Economics*, *19*(1), 113–121.

Ford, J. (2005). Examining leadership through critical feminist readings. *Journal of Health Organization and Management*, *19*(3), 236–251.

Fox, S., & Gregory, D. (2004). Gender, HR and the line in construction. *Employee Relations*, 26(2), 123–139.

Gale, A. W. (1992a). Women in non-traditional occupations: The construction industry. *Women in Management Review*, 9, 33–14.

Gale, A. W. (1992b). *The construction industry's male culture must feminize if conflict is to be reduced: The role of education as a gatekeeper to a male construction industry.*

Gale, A. W. (1994). Women in non-traditional occupations: The construction industry. *Women in Management Review*, 9(2), 3–14.

Gale, A., & Davidson, M. (2006). Women in refuge: Work, hom(e) and asylum in housing after domestic violence. *Work, Employment & Society*, 20(1), 51–75.

Gardner, H. (1995). *Leading minds*. Harper Collins.

Ghana Statistical Service. (2019). Ghana living standards survey (GLSS) round 7. [online]. www.statsghana.gov.gh. Accessed on 5 August 2023.

Giritli, H., & Oraz, T. (2004). Leadership styles: Some evidence from the Turkish construction industry. *Construction Management & Economics*, 22, 253–262.

Giritli, H. N., & Oraz, G. T. (2004). Leadership styles: Some evidence from the Turkish construction industry. *Construction Management & Economics*, 22(3), 253–262. https://doi.org/10.1080/0144619042000148173

Goldman, D., & Cropanzano, R. (2015). "Justice" and the challenge of integrating ethics and psychology. *Annual Review of Psychology*, 66, 583–605. https://doi.org/10.1146/annurev-psych-010814-015156

Goleman, D. (2000, March–April) Leadership that gets results. *Harvard Business Review*, 78–90.

Gouthro, M. B., John, S., & Perrault, S. (2008). Gender and participation in continuing professional education: A Canadian study of accountants. *Gender in Management: An International Journal*, 23(8), 579–593.

Greckol, S. (1987). *Women into construction*. National Association for Women in Construction.

Greed, C. (2000). Women in the construction professions: A fair share of the building? *Women in Management Review*, 15(2), 52–61.

Gurjao, S. (2008). *Inclusiveness: Changing role of women in the construction workforce.* Chartered Institute of Building (CIOB).

Hackman, M., Hills, A. H., & Paterson, T. J. (1992). Perceptions of gender-role characteristics and transformational and transactional leadership behaviours. *Perceptual and Motor Skills, 75,* 311–319.

Halligan, M., Healey, B., & Murray, J. P. (2008). Social-cognitive and neuropsychological aspects of reactive aggression: Models and mechanisms. In R. J. Boddezsky (Ed.), *Managing aggressive behaviour in care settings* (pp. 25–52). Jessica Kingsley Publishers.

Harrison, J. (2010). (Re) constructing a glass ceiling? Women and leadership in civil engineering organisations. *Women in Management Review, 25*(2), 119–136.

Heike, A., Mavunye, N., & Hinga, C. (2017). Women empowerment in the South African construction industry. *Procedia Engineering, 196,* 108–114.

Hezlett, S. A., & Gibson, S. K. (2022). Mentoring and human resource development: A review of the literature. *Journal of Management, 24*(3), 449–467.

Hillebrandt, P. M. (1985). *Analysis of the building process.* Granada Publishing Limited.

Hofstede, G. H. (1998). *Masculinity and femininity: The taboo dimension of national cultures.* Sage.

Hofstede, G. (2001). *Culture' consequences: Comparing values, behaviours, institutions, and organizations across nations* (2nd ed.). Sage Publications.

Horwitz, A. V. (2007). A sociological perspective on the experience of distress. *Psychiatric Services, 58*(4), 448–450.

Ikpoto, & Nonyelum, C. A. (2015). Adopting mentorship programs as a strategy for career development of subordinates: A literature review. *Journal of Business and Management, 17*(6), 8–19.

Johnson, L. M. (2021a). Gender inequality in the construction sector: Challenges and opportunities. *Construction Management Review, 10*(2), 45–60.

Johnson, L. M. (2021b). Employment diversity in the construction sector: A comprehensive review. *Construction Employment Journal, 10*(2), 78–92.

Johnson, L. M. (2021c). Allocation of financial resources for gender equality programmes in the construction industry: A framework for change. *Construction Resources Quarterly, 20*(2), 45–60.

Johnson, L. M. (2021d). Women networking and mentoring programs in the construction industry: Promoting gender equality. *Construction Leadership Forum, 18*(2), 60–75.

Johnson, L. M. (2021e). Women's safety orientation in the construction industry: A comparative analysis. *Construction Safety Journal, 10*(3), 45–60.

Jome, L. M., Surething, N. A., & Taylor, J. K. (2006). Career maturity and preferences in business and engineering students: A comparative analysis. *Journal of Business and Psychology, 20*(3), 457–468.

Kalbfleisch, P. J., & Keyton, J. (2018). Gender differences in mentoring experiences: A literature review. *Gender and Mentoring Research Journal, 10*(2), 78–92.

Kanter, R. M. (1993). *Men and women of the corporation* (2nd ed.). Basic Books.

Kark, R. (2004). The transformational leader: Who is (s)he? A feminist perspective. *Journal of Organisational Change Management, 17*(2), 160–176.

Klenke, K. (1996). *Women and leadership: A contextual perspective.* Springer.

Kram, K. E. (2018a). Mentoring in the construction industry: A literature review. *Construction Industry Mentorship Journal, 10*(2), 78–92.

Kram, K. E. (2018b). Importance of mentoring in the South African construction industry: A case study. *South African Construction Review, 25*(1), 30–45.

Kram, K. E. (2018c). *Mentoring at work: Developmental relationships in organizational life.* University Press.

Kram, K. E. (2018d). Workplace mentoring and its impact on employee performance. *Journal of Organizational Psychology, 30*(2), 89–104.

Langford, D., Fellows, R. F., Hancock, M., & Gale, A. W. (1995). Human resource management in construction, Longman scientific and technical.

Lawless, J. (2001). Women, war and victory: A female secondary head teachers in England and Wales. *School Leadership & Management*, 21(1), 75–84.

Larson, A., & Freeman, R. E. (1997). Introduction. In A. Larson & R. E. Freeman (Eds.), *Women's studies and business ethics: Toward a new conversation* (pp. 3–10). Oxford University Press.

Lingard, H., & Francis, V. (2004). The work-life experiences of office and site-based employees in the Australian construction industry. *Construction Management & Economics*, 22(9), 991–1002.

Lingard, H. C., & Francis, V. (2004). The work-life experiences of construction personnel in Australia and the UK. *Construction Management & Economics*, 22(4), 391–402.

Lingard, H., & Lin, J. (2002). Career, family and work environment determinants of organisational commitment among women in the Australian construction industry. *Construction Management & Economics*, 20(4), 409–420.

Lopez, M. J. (2023). Sociocultural influences on developing nations' construction industries. *International Journal of Construction Studies*, 7(2), 89–102.

Lu, W., Li, J., & Yang, P. (2017). Comparing the impacts of BIM and conventional delivery approaches in construction. *Journal of Construction Engineering and Management*, 143(2), 4016026.

Naum, S. (2011). *People and organisational management in construction* (2nd ed.). ICE.

Nguyen, T. (2016). A framework for proactive construction defect management using BIM, augmented reality and ontology-based data collection template. *Automation in Construction*, 63, 37–49.

Northouse, P. G. (2004). *Leadership theory and practice*. Sage Publications.

Okewole, I. (1997). Male-female cooperative approach to shelter development in Nigeria. In *Proceedings of a national symposium on the house in Nigeria, Ile-Ife, Nigeria* (pp. 93–96).

Olanipekun, E., & Ogunduyile, D. (2011). Barriers to effective participation of women in the Nigerian construction industry. In *ASC annual international conference proceedings, Cancun, Mexico*.

Olaoluwa, J., & Ajala, E. (2011). Effects of construction education on participation of women in Nigeria's construction industry. In *ASC annual international conference proceedings, Cancun, Mexico.*

Oliveira-Filho, A. B., Aires, D. W. F., Cavalcante, N. S., Costa Raiol, N., Lisboa, B. L. A., Frade, P. C. R., da Costa, L. M., Pinheiro, L. M. L., Machado, L. F. A., Martins, L. C., Silva-Oliveira, G. C., Pinho, J. R. R., Kupek, E., & Lemos, J. R. R. (2015). *Gender differences in project management.*

Olofsson, B. (2000). Kvinnor i byggyrken- en kombination av kvinnor och män på byggen. *Construction Management & Economics, 18*(5), 539–547.

Orrwari, Y. (1992). The role of women in housing finance: A case study of Port Harcout, Nigeria. In *Paper presented at the fifth international research conference on housing, Montreal.*

Orubuloye, I. (1987). Values and costs of daughters and sons of Yoruba mothers and fathers. In C. Oppong (Ed.), *Sex roles, population and development in West Africa* (pp. 86–90). Heineman Educational Books Inc.

Pheng, L. S., & Lee, B. S. K. (1997) East meets West: Leadership development for construction project management. *Journal of Managerial Psychology, 12*(6), 383–400.

Powell, A., Bagilhole, B., Dainty, A., & Neale, R. (2005) Coping in construction: Female students' perspectives. In *Paper presented at proceedings 21st annual ARCOM conference, technology for development (IASTED), Cartagena, Colombia.*

Ragins, B. R., & Cotton, J. L. (2021). Easier Said than done: Gender differences in perceived barriers to gaining a mentor. *Academy of Management Journal, 39*(2), 525–548.

Rochlen, A. B., Mohr, J. J., & Hargrove, B. K. (1999). Development of the attitudes toward career counseling scale. *Journal of Counseling Psychology, 46*(2), 196.

Rosener, J. B. (1990). Ways women lead. (cover story). *Harvard Business Review, 68*(6), 119–125.

Sekaran, U. (2003). *Research methods for business: A skill building approach* (4th ed.). John Wiley & Sons.

Shin, S. J. (1994). Effects of career-type and gender-typed attributes on career achievement. *Sex Roles, 31*(3–4), 145–154.

Smith, J. K. (2022a). Barriers to women's participation in the construction industry: A qualitative analysis. *Journal of Gender Studies in Construction, 15*(3), 78–92.

Smith, J. K. (2022b). Integrating a culture of diversity in the construction workplace: Best practices and strategies. *Workplace Diversity Management, 25*(1), 30–45.

Smith, J. K. (2022c). Women's roles in construction: From non-management to leadership positions. *Gender and Construction Work Review, 20*(3), 45–60.

Smith, J. K. (2022d). Women in managerial positions: Trends and implications for the construction industry. *Management Review, 25*(1), 30–45.

Smith, J. K. (2022e). Gender disparities in mentoring functions: Implications for female proteges. *Gender and Career Development Quarterly, 15*(4), 110–125.

Smith, J. K., & Johnson, L. M. (2022). Gender mainstreaming initiatives in construction policy: A government perspective. *Construction Policy Journal, 15*(3), 78–92.

Sokomba, M. T. (1990). The participation of women in design and construction of housing stock in Nigeria. In *Proceedings of the Nigerian indigenous building materials symposium, Ahmadu Bello University, Zaria* (pp. 213–237).

Townley, B. (1989). Piece rate. In R. J. B. Creighton (Ed.), *Knowledge and power in Colliery districts: Community and conflict in North-East Lancashire before 1914*. Cambridge University Press.

Twenge, J. M. (2020). Diminishing gender effects in mentoring: A contemporary perspective. *Contemporary Mentoring Trends Review, 20*(3), 45–60.

Wang, S. H. (2021). Gender bias in the construction industry: A sociocultural perspective. *Construction Diversity Review, 15*(3), 45–60.

Wells, J. (1990). The role of women in the construction industry. *Construction Management & Economics, 8*, 3–7.

Wentling, R. M. (1996). Work-family conflict in dual-career families. Virginia Tech: Women in International Development, Mary Baldwin College Web site. http://www.wm.edu/AS/workfamily. Accessed on 12 October 2006.

Whittock, M. (2002). Women's experiences of non-traditional employment: Is gender equality in this area a possibility? *Construction Management & Economics, 20,* 449–456.

Witt, L., & Nye, L. (1998). Gender and the relationship between perceived fairness of performance evaluation and organizational outcomes. *Journal of Applied Psychology, 78,* 850–855.

World Bank. (1994). *Nigeria: Strategies for building the private sector.* World Bank.

5

EMPOWERING WOMEN: PERSPECTIVE OF EUROPE, ASIA AND AFRICA

ABSTRACT

This is the last part of the book, and it highlights the international perspective of women's empowerment in construction. The chapter also captures women's participation in the context of European, Asian, African and other continents. Essential factors influencing women's empowerment and involvement in the construction industry have also been considered.

Keywords: Africa; Asia; empowerment; Europe; international; women

1. INTRODUCTION

Encouraging women to work in construction is a global endeavour that necessitates a thorough comprehension of the distinct viewpoints and obstacles encountered in various areas. In this section of the book, the viewpoints of Europe, Asia and Africa regarding the promotion of gender equality in the construction industry are examined. The construction industry may benefit from a more diverse and inclusive work environment that allows women to grow, contribute and progress without encountering barriers based on their gender. This is what it means to empower women in the sector. Collaboration between individuals, organisations and policymakers is necessary for this comprehensive approach. Establishing an atmosphere where women have equal opportunity, representation and support to flourish both personally and professionally within the business is essential to empowering women in the construction sector. This empowerment may take many different forms. Guaranteeing equal opportunities for women in the workplace, in terms of promotions and career growth, relative to men. This entails eliminating gender prejudice and ensuring fairness in the hiring and advancement procedures. It is essential to cultivate an inclusive and diverse working atmosphere. Promoting respect, combating discrimination and fostering an environment where women feel valued, accepted and capable of making meaningful contributions are all part of this. Granting women the same chances for education and training in sectors related to building. This may entail promoting science, technology, engineering and mathematics education and career training for girls and young women. Endorsing and defending legislative and institutional measures that advance gender parity in the construction sector. This comprises programmes that target systemic impediments, such as affirmative action policies and anti-discrimination policies. Ensuring that occupational health and safety policies take into account the unique requirements and welfare of women. This entails offering suitable facilities, attending to personal safety issues and taking health concerns into account.

2. OVERVIEW OF WOMEN IN THE EUROPEAN CONSTRUCTION CONTEXT

Progressive laws have been put in place in several European nations to support gender equality in the workplace, particularly in the construction sector. Europe's construction industry has historically been dominated by men, with little prospects for women to participate or progress in the field. Women are discouraged from pursuing professions in construction because of traditional gender roles and preconceptions that typically equate the industry with physical labour and masculinity. These regulations prioritise possibilities for job progression, parental leave and fair pay. European countries frequently place a strong emphasis on Science, Technology, Engineering and Mathematics education that is gender-neutral. This encourages young females to seek jobs in industries that have historically been dominated by men, like construction. Networking and mentorship programmes that connect women in construction, offer a support system, and promote professional development have become more popular in Europe.

2.1 Factors Affecting Women's Empowerment in Europe

The process of empowering women in Europe is complex and influenced by several factors, including social standards, political representation, economic

engagement and education. A more equal and empowered society for women
will result from ongoing efforts to address these concerns. The European
construction industry, traditionally male-dominated, is transforming greater
gender diversity. Achieving women's empowerment in this sector involves
navigating a range of factors that impact recruitment, retention and professional development. This part explores key elements influencing women's
empowerment in the European construction industry, analysing policies, cultural dynamics and industry-specific initiatives. The process of empowering
women in the European construction sector is complex and includes lobbying
work, workplace policies, industry-specific initiatives and cultural shifts. The
construction industry may foster a work climate where women feel empowered to fully participate and succeed in their careers by tackling these factors
holistically. Women's empowerment and health and well-being are intimately
related. A woman's total empowerment is influenced by her access to mental
health treatments, reproductive rights and healthcare resources. European
nations with extensive healthcare systems frequently demonstrate elevated
degrees of female empowerment. To empower women, they must actively
participate in the workforce. Economic independence is fostered by policies
that support work-life balance, and equal pay, and address occupational
segregation. In Europe, progressive laws and business campaigns have sought
to lessen gender differences in the workplace. Being involved in industry
groups and women's networks helps to build relationships, provides a forum
for exchanging experiences and increases the visibility of women in the construction business.

Development is greatly aided by women, who are a valuable resource in the
labour market in Europe. There are several issues facing the increasing number
of women employed in the industrial sector, particularly about the calibre of
their human capital. Labour productivity is one way to gauge the calibre of
human resources. Human resources with higher qualifications will be more
productive than those with lower qualifications. The community's perceptions
of the value of education for both men and women, as well as the growing
recognition of the necessity of women's involvement in development, have led
to an increase in the number of housewives who work in family economic
operations. Community perceptions and attitudes on the value of education
for both men and women have changed, and women's participation in
development is becoming increasingly recognized. Housewives' willingness to
be self-sufficient in the financial sphere is demonstrated by their attempt to
meet their dependents' necessities.

Enhancing the well-being of the entire community is the goal of women's
empowerment. Considering that women concurrently fulfill two responsibilities.

To give women and their groups a business foundation, the networks that are developed must be strengthened. Members of the organisation should possess the fortitude to face a brighter future. Initiating and executing collaboration with numerous entities is vital, particularly with non-governmental organisations (NGOs) operating at the regional level, to facilitate the formation of a cooperative business network. To provide the community with the most influence over decision-making, cooperation is practiced. Additionally, to relieve women of their oppression resulting from discriminatory treatment by various parties in the political, economic, sociocultural and legal spheres, as well as to increase and actualise their potential and make them more capable of being independent and employed, empowerment of women is necessary. Furthermore, it is imperative to enhance the assimilation and implementation of technology as a tactic for enabling women in all developmental processes via enhanced education, training and skill development, as well as relevant and inventive technologies.

2.2 Women's Contribution to the Construction Industry in Europe

There has been a paradigm shift in the construction business in Europe in recent years, with a growing number of women making significant contributions to the field. Traditionally, men have controlled the construction industry. This part of the book highlights women's significant achievements, obstacles they have faced and initiatives to further gender diversity and inclusivity in the European construction sector. A growing number of women are working on architectural and design-related building projects. Their original concepts and imaginative input enhance the infrastructures and buildings' visual attractiveness and use. More and more women are taking on leadership positions in project management and managing intricate building projects from start to finish. Their attention to detail and organisational abilities are essential for guaranteeing the timely and effective implementation of building plans. In the past male-dominated technical and engineering fields, women broke down barriers. Their proficiency in mechanical, structural and civil engineering adds variety to the technical facets of building projects. On construction sites, women are actively involved in promoting and putting safety precautions into place. Their efforts address long-standing worries about employees' well-being and contribute to the creation of safer work environments. Women are contributing significantly to the European construction industry by bringing a variety of viewpoints, talents and innovations to the field. Even while there has been progress, more has to be done to remove obstacles and provide equitable opportunities for women in the construction industry. The construction sector can keep reaping the rewards of women's skills and capacities by encouraging education, dispelling myths and creating welcoming environments. The diverse, significant and indispensable contributions made by women to the European construction industry are crucial for promoting inclusion, sustainability and innovation in the field. Women play important roles in influencing the built environment, expanding building techniques and fostering diversity and inclusion in the industry, despite confronting obstacles to their participation and success. Europe can fully utilise the potential of women in construction to propel economic growth, social progress and sustainable development in the area by appreciating the contributions made by women, advocating for gender equality and policies that support it and cultivating an inclusive and mentoring culture. Europe can establish a more gender-neutral society by persisting in dismantling gender stereotypes, removing obstacles to women's involvement, and providing chances for women to lead and prosper in the construction sector.

2.3 Mentorship of Women in Construction in the European Context

In the European construction industry, mentoring programmes have become essential instruments for women's advancement in this historically male-dominated field. Mentoring is fundamental to professional development. This fragment of the book points to the value of mentorship programmes in empowering and assisting women working in construction throughout Europe, looking at their advantages, difficulties and noteworthy projects. Through individualised advice on career paths, skill development and industry intricacies, mentoring gives women in the construction sector a valuable advantage. Mentors are important sources of guidance and support, assisting mentees in overcoming obstacles and coming to wise judgements. Gender stereotypes are a persistent problem in the construction business. Women can flourish in a variety of areas within the industry thanks to mentoring programmes, which provide a forum for challenging and dispelling these preconceptions.

Skilled mentors impart their knowledge and experience, allowing the transfer of skills relevant to the sector. Making sure that women in construction have access to the skills necessary for success and closing the gender gap depends on this transfer of information. The growth of networking abilities and confidence – two things that are necessary for job advancement – are

facilitated by mentoring connections. Women in construction can broaden
their professional networks and develop the self-assurance necessary to succeed in leadership positions through mentoring. Jobs in the construction sector
sometimes involve strict deadlines. Mentors can offer insightful guidance on
striking a healthy work–life balance, assisting women in overcoming the difficulties of balancing personal and professional obligations. Even with the
benefits of mentoring programmes, issues like lack of understanding, unconscious bias and restricted access to mentors still exist. Employers, academic
institutions, professional associations and other industry stakeholders must
work together to find solutions to these problems. In the European construction sector, mentoring programmes are essential to the development and
success of female professionals. These programmes help create a more diverse
and inclusive construction industry by offering advice, dismantling obstacles
and promoting skill development. Initiatives for mentoring women in the
European construction sector are in various forms.

To encourage women to explore and advance in science, technology,
engineering and mathematics–related occupations, including those in the
construction sector, Women into Science and Engineering in the United
Kingdom offers mentorship programmes and initiatives. Additionally, the
European Institute for Gender Equality (EIGE) advocates for gender equality
in several industries, including construction. The institution helps to create
mentoring programmes by funding studies and projects that address gender
disparities. National Association of Women in Construction (NAWIC)
mentorship programmes operate in various European countries. Throughout
Europe, NAWIC in the European chapters frequently hosts mentorship programmes that pair seasoned professionals with women starting or making
success in the construction business. To address gender imbalances, promote
diversity and inclusion and create a welcoming and inclusive work environment within the construction industry, mentoring programmes for women in
construction are essential in Europe. These mentorship programmes enable
women to overcome obstacles, handle career problems and realize their full
potential in the construction sector by offering advice, support and chances for
skill development and networking. Europe can leverage the skills and contributions of women to propel innovation, sustainability and excellence in the
construction industry by extending mentorship opportunities, advocating for
gender equality and cultivating an inclusive and supportive culture. Mentorship programmes act as catalysts for positive change, giving women the confidence to lead and prosper in the construction industry.

3. OVERVIEW OF WOMEN IN THE CONSTRUCTION
ASIAN CONTEXT

The formerly male-dominated Asian construction sector is undergoing a radical change as more and more women are lending their knowledge and experience to the field. This section of the book examines women's status in the construction industry in several Asian nations, highlighting obstacles encountered and efforts to advance gender diversity. Gender prejudices and cultural conventions can be major obstacles for women wanting to work in construction in various Asian nations. There is a push to break these conventions and establish more welcoming settings. Several Asian nations have launched skill development initiatives to provide women with the technical know-how required for construction jobs (European Commission, 2020). The goal of these programmes is to close the knowledge and certification gap between genders. Realizing the financial advantages of having a gender-balanced staff, some Asian construction businesses are proactively promoting diversity and inclusion. Many Asian nations struggle with deeply embedded cultural norms and stereotypes that support the notion that some occupations, like building, are the purview of men. Encouraging diversity requires overcoming these cultural obstacles. A growing number of initiatives are concentrating on developing skills. The Malaysian Construction Industry Development Board provides technical skills to women to prepare them for careers in construction.

There are initiatives in India to dispel prejudices and cultural conventions. Advocates and organisations are trying to shift attitudes and inspire more women to enter the construction industry. It is becoming more common for women to work in Japan's construction business over time. Roscigno and Hodson (2004) opined that businesses that understand the value of having a diverse workforce, such as Shimizu Corporation, are actively participating in diversity and inclusion efforts. One well-known example of a business actively fostering diversity and inclusion is Shimizu Corporation in Japan. Among its policies are initiatives to foster an inclusive workplace atmosphere that rewards workers of all genders (Sen, 2001). South Korea is taking action to close the gender gap in the building industry. The study by Sen (2001) pointed out that promoting equal chances and combating gender prejudice in hiring procedures are two initiatives. South Korean construction firms are putting rules in place to support women's involvement in the sector as they become more aware of the advantages of having a diverse workforce. Through skill development programmes, the Malaysian Construction Industry Development Board empowers women and encourages them to seek jobs in construction

(Sen, 2001). Singapore on the other hand is funding educational and training initiatives to provide women with the tools they need to work in construction. The goal of initiatives is to remove barriers linked to gender in the sector.

3.1 Factors That Influence Women's Empowerment in Asia

Women's empowerment in Asia is a diverse phenomenon that is influenced by political, social, economic and cultural factors. To achieve gender equality and sustainable development in the region, it is crucial to empower women. Education plays a role in empowering women as it equips them with the skills and knowledge to participate in the workforce. Offering employment opportunities and providing support for women-owned businesses contribute to their independence and decision-making abilities, which are aspects of empowerment. Implementing laws and policies that address violence against women and gender discrimination is crucial for promoting women's empowerment. Increased representation of women in politics amplifies their influence and contributes to the creation of inclusive legislation.

Challenging expectations and traditional gender roles are necessary for progress to occur. In countries, family dynamics can influence women's autonomy and decision-making within their homes. Access to technology empowers women by providing avenues for learning, communication and entrepreneurship that can have impacts on their social and economic status. Challenging and modifying these traditions is crucial for progress. The way families are structured and function in societies can influence the level of autonomy and decision-making power that women have within their households.

3.2 Women's Contribution to the Construction Industry in Asia

Although the construction business in Asia has traditionally been associated with men, a growing number of women are breaking preconceptions, making important contributions and changing the landscape of the industry. The industry's talent pool is expanding as more and more Asian women are going to school and receiving training in disciplines like engineering, design and construction management. By holding positions like project manager, surveyor, engineer and architect, women are shattering stereotypes and advancing the technical and managerial facets of the field. Women offer distinct viewpoints on the design process, impacting choices about architecture and building with an emphasis on sustainability, usability and beauty. Women-led teams encourage innovation in building techniques, materials and technology, which produces more cost-effective and ecologically friendly solutions. Construction industry workers who identify as women frequently support community-focused initiatives, which help create safer and more environmentally friendly living environments (Lilian, 2015). Women in leadership positions are pushing for social responsibility in the construction sector by putting a focus on community involvement, fair labour standards and ethical procedures. Women still encounter prejudice and discrimination in the construction sector despite advancements. These issues must be resolved to establish a diverse and equal workplace.

Sustained efforts are required to improve women's access to skill development and training programmes, so they may fulfil their duties with excellence. The presence of women is challenging conventional conventions and promoting diversity, resulting in a change towards more welcoming and supportive work cultures. Programmes that encourage networking and mentoring are assisting women in the construction sector in overcoming obstacles, seizing opportunities and advancing in their professions.

3.3 Mentorship of Women in the Construction in Asia Context

Encouraging women in the Asian continent's construction sector through mentoring is essential. Mentorship programmes give women professionals tremendous support, direction and chances to grow in their professions, overcome obstacles and make a positive impact on an increasingly diverse industry as the sector continues to change. Mentorship programmes create networks for knowledge sharing, cooperation and career progress by putting women in the workforce in contact with leaders in the field. Through a venue for exchanging experiences, perspectives and techniques for overcoming obstacles in a male-dominated field, mentoring gives women a sense of empowerment and camaraderie. Mentors provide direction and knowledge to support women in gaining technical proficiency, leadership qualities and self-assurance in their employment in the construction industry. Through helping women develop goals for their careers, find growth opportunities and manage professional changes, mentoring improves their long-term chances in the field. Inspiring upcoming generations of women to seek jobs in construction, female mentors act as role models and champions for diversity and inclusion in the sector. Through mentoring programmes, gender prejudices and biases are challenged, giving women in construction organisations a chance to rise to leadership roles and participate in decision-making. Mentors help manage family duties and strike a work–life balance, addressing the particular difficulties women have in juggling work and domestic obligations. Through mentoring, women can navigate and overcome prejudices, discrimination and gender bias that are common in the construction business, enabling them to achieve success on their own terms. When construction companies, universities and trade groups work together, mentorship programmes are strengthened and opportunities for women professionals are increased. Development and sustainability of mentorship programmes for women in construction across Asia are facilitated by policy efforts and government funding support.

4. OVERVIEW OF WOMEN IN CONSTRUCTION AFRICAN CONTEXT

The empowerment of women in the African construction industry is mostly dependent on economic empowerment. This comprises programmes that offer tools, training and financial assistance to female entrepreneurs just starting in the field. To dispel prejudices and gain support for women seeking professions in construction, many African projects incorporate community participation and awareness campaigns (O'Reilly, 2015). A few African nations have enacted laws and policies that support gender parity in the workplace to foster an atmosphere that allows women to prosper in the construction industry.

In Africa, women contribute significantly to infrastructure development, economic growth and community empowerment in the construction industry despite their often-overlooked roles. Women in Africa are breaking down boundaries and achieving success in a variety of construction-related industries despite encountering many obstacles. To help construct buildings, roads, bridges and other infrastructure projects, women in Africa actively engage in specialised crafts like carpentry, plumbing, electrical work and masonry. More and more women are working as project managers, supervising building projects from inception to conclusion while showcasing their leadership and organizational abilities. Numerous African women own small-scale construction companies, specialising in tasks like painting, roofing, interior design and bricklaying. These enterprises promote regional economic growth and job creation. Women-owned construction companies give women economic power by giving them possibilities for skill development and training, financial independence and decision-making authority. Pervasive cultural norms and gender stereotypes frequently prevent women from pursuing leadership roles, training programmes and jobs in the construction industry, which perpetuates gender inequality. Women are unable to compete on an equal basis with males in the construction business because they lack access to financial resources, education, training and supportive networks. This makes it difficult for women to participate in and grow in the field.

4.1 Factors That Influence Women's Empowerment in Africa

Social progress and sustainable development in Africa are significantly influenced by the empowerment of women. On the other hand, to truly empower women throughout the continent, several interrelated issues must be addressed. Having access to education is essential to women's empowerment. Inequalities in access to education persist throughout much of Africa, where girls face obstacles such as early marriage, cultural traditions that prioritise boys' education and poverty. Girls who receive a high-quality education are better equipped to participate more actively in the social and economic realms because it increases their agency, knowledge and skill sets (Kabeer, 2005). For women to have autonomy and decision-making capacity, economic empowerment is essential. Obstacles to women's economic engagement include unequal compensation, discriminatory labour practices and restricted credit availability (Gusti & Made, 2019). Proposals that encourage entrepreneurship, vocational training and financial services accessibility can enable women economically and aid in the fight against poverty. Traditional customs and deeply ingrained cultural norms frequently support gender inequity. Women are less autonomous and have fewer possibilities due to practices including female genital mutilation, early marriage and rigid gender norms. Encouraging gender-equitable attitudes and behaviours requires working to dismantle detrimental conventions via activism, education and community involvement. Situations of conflict and humanitarian aid present particular obstacles to women's empowerment and worsen gender disparities. When there are conflicts, women and girls are frequently more vulnerable to violence, displacement and loss of livelihood. Women's rights in conflict-affected areas must be advanced by attending to their unique requirements in humanitarian operations, encouraging their involvement in peacebuilding initiatives and guaranteeing their access to justice and protection. Women's representation in political decision-making processes remains low across many African countries. Structural barriers such as limited access to political positions, patriarchal political systems and cultural biases against women in leadership roles hinder women's political empowerment. Increasing women's participation in politics through quota systems, affirmative action measures and leadership training programmes can enhance their voice and influence in shaping policies and governance (Gusti & Made, 2019).

To address the complex factors that contribute to women's empowerment, intersectional and holistic methods are needed. These approaches should address structural injustices at their root and advance women's agency, rights and opportunities in a range of contexts. Encouraging sustained progress towards gender equality in Africa requires cooperation between governments, the corporate sector, civil society organizations and international partners.

4.2 Women's Contribution to the Construction Industry in Africa

Though sometimes disregarded or undervalued, women make a substantial contribution to the African construction industry. Construction has always been a male-dominated field, but in recent years, women have begun to play a wider range of responsibilities in all facets of the business. Their roles are varied, ranging from manual labour to managerial roles, and they play a crucial role in advancing gender equality, sustainable development and economic progress (Lilian, 2015). This is a thorough summary of the contributions and effects of women in the African construction industry. Within the construction business, women in Africa actively engage in skilled trades and manual labour. They contribute to the construction of residential buildings, commercial projects and building infrastructure by working as masons, carpenters, plumbers, electricians and painters, among other jobs. Many women succeed in these historically male-dominated industries, demonstrating their resiliency and skillfulness, despite encountering preconceptions and physical obstacles. In the construction industry, women's advocacy groups and professional associations fight for equal opportunity, safe working conditions and gender parity. They encourage inclusive legislation, create support networks for women employed in the construction industry and increase public awareness of gender-based discrimination (Kochan et al., 2003). Through the amplification of female voices and experiences, these organisations aid in the development of a more inclusive and fair construction sector. Across the continent, women architects and engineers are actively involved in the planning, designing and managing of building projects. Their knowledge aids in the creation of robust infrastructure, sustainable designs and creative solutions. Women professionals are significantly impacting the built environment in Africa despite obstacles such as gender bias and restricted access to senior positions (Kuras, 2019).

The construction business in Africa has witnessed a noteworthy and varied contribution from women, who are vital in propelling the sector's expansion and advancement throughout the continent. But to further empower women in the construction sector, issues like gender stereotypes, restricted access to training and education and workplace discrimination still need to be addressed.

4.3 Mentorship of Women in the Construction Industry in Africa

Research and business insights highlight the vital importance of mentorship for women in the construction sector. Accordingly, Liu and Fellows (2018) stressed that given the distinct opportunities and problems that women in Africa confront in the construction business, mentoring women in this sector is especially important. In Africa, mentoring is essential to the advancement of women's careers in the building sector (Chileshe et al., 2018). Due to the field's historical male dominance, women frequently encounter particular difficulties and obstacles to entry and advancement. Mentoring programmes provide invaluable possibilities for skill development, networking and empowerment as well as support and direction. This is a comprehensive examination of the value of mentoring for women in the African construction sector. Mentorship programmes are crucial for empowering and assisting women in Africa's construction sector. Chiu and Ling (2018) opined that mentorship plays a significant role in fostering a more diverse, inclusive and equitable construction industry by offering access to opportunities, skill development, confidence building, networking, progression pathways and cultural transformation. Mentorship programmes are essential in helping women stay in the construction business because they provide a sense of support, community and career fulfilment (Liu & Fellows, 2018). The likelihood that mentees would stay interested, motivated and dedicated to their jobs in the face of challenges and disappointments is higher when they get mentorship and assistance. The establishment of welcoming and encouraging work cultures that support gender equality and diversity is facilitated by mentoring. Establishing professional connections and networking are crucial for career progression in the construction sector, and mentoring helps with these tasks. To foster chances for mentorship, collaboration and future career prospects, mentors can connect mentees with important stakeholders, business leaders and possible partners. Mentoring facilitates networking and provides doors to new collaborations, projects and career paths.

Women's career advancement and success in the construction sector in Africa can be greatly aided by mentoring programmes that foster diversity and inclusion, address gender imbalances and support women (Ling & Chiu, 2018). These programmes enable women to overcome obstacles, negotiate career problems and realize their full potential in the construction industry by offering mentorship, coaching and chances for skill development and networking, Liu and Fellows (2018) indicate that expanding mentorship programmes, maximising their impact and establishing institutional support systems for gender equality and inclusion in the construction sector require partnerships, collaborations and policy assistance. Africa can fully utilise women's talents and contributions to propel sustainable development, economic growth and social advancement in the region by making a concentrated effort to support women's leadership and participation in the construction industry.

BIBLIOGRAPHY

African Development Bank. (2020). *Construction sector: Women in construction.*

African Development Bank Group (ADBG). (2019). *Women in the African construction industry: Challenges, opportunities, and the way forward.*

Agutu, S. M., & Karugu, J. W. (2020). Women in the construction industry in Kenya: Opportunities, challenges and prospects. *International Journal of Science and Research (IJSR)*, 9(11), 1661–1667.

Ajuzie, H. D., Mohammed, C. A., & Alhaji, D. (2012). Assessment of the influence of education on women empowerment: Implication for national development. *European Journal of Globalization and Development, Department of Educational Foundation*, 6(1), 1304–1327.

Al-Hegami, A. S., & Mbachu, J. (2018). Women's participation in the construction industry in Saudi Arabia: Challenges and opportunities. *Built Environment Project and Asset Management*, 8(2), 146–162.

Amole, D. (2019). Women in construction: A neglected group in Nigeria. *The Nigerian Builder*, 8(1), 24–27.

Chakraborty, S., & Joshi, S. (2018). Women's empowerment in India: Issues, challenges, and strategies. *Social Change*, 48(3), 435–457.

Chileshe, N., Rambau, L., & Haupt, T. C. (2018). Gender diversity in the construction industry: A case of South Africa. *Journal of Engineering, Design and Technology, 16*(4), 566–584.

Chiu, Y. H., & Ling, F. Y. Y. (2018). The role of mentoring in enhancing female engineers' career success in the construction industry. *International Journal of Construction Management, 18*(5), 370–382.

CITB. (2021). *Women in construction: Industry factsheet.*

Construction Industry Development Board Malaysia. (2020). *Women in construction: Unlocking opportunities.*

European Commission. (2021). *Gender equality in the workplace.*

European Commission. (2022). *Women in transport – EU platform for change.*

European Institute for Gender Equality. (2017). *Gender Equality Index 2017: Measuring gender-based discrimination and promoting gender equality.*

European Institute for Gender Equality. (2020). *Gender Equality Index 2020 – Sweden.*

European Institute for Gender Equality. (2022). *Gender equality in the construction sector in Europe.*

Gan, Y., & Chen, Y. (2019). A qualitative exploration of the career barriers and facilitators for women in the construction industry in China. *Construction Management and Economics, 37*(8), 452–466.

Gusti, A. P., & Made, S. U. (2019, February). Women's empowerment strategies to improve their role in families and society. *International Journal of Business, Economics, and Law, 18*(5). ISSN 2289-1552.

Hall, R., & Mclaughlin, P. (2011). Women in the construction industry: Breaking down the barriers. *Engineering, Construction and Architectural Management, 18*(2), 130–143.

International Labour Organization. (2019). *Women in construction sector: Opportunities and challenges for developing countries.*

International Labour Organization. (2021). *Advancing gender equality in the world of work.*

Kabeer, N. (2005). Gender equality and women's empowerment: A critical analysis of the third Millennium Development Goal 1. *Gender & Development, 13*(1), 13–24.

Kochan, T., Bezrukova, K., Ely, R., Jackson, S., Joshi, A., Jehn, K., & Thomas, D. (2003). The effects of diversity on business performance: Report of the diversity research network. *Human Resource Management, 42*(1), 3–21.

Kuras, M. (2019). *Women in construction: An investigation into the experiences of women in the construction industry in Europe.* European Institute for Gender Equality (EIGE).

Lilian, A. (2015). Women and the construction industry in Africa: Challenges and opportunities. *Proceedings of the Institution of Civil Engineers-Municipal Engineer, 168*(1), 17–26.

Ling, F. Y. Y., & Chiu, Y. H. (2018). Exploring the relationship between mentoring functions and career success among female engineers in the construction industry. *Journal of Engineering, Design, and Technology, 16*(6), 1026–1043.

Liu, A. M. M., & Fellows, R. F. (2018). Role of mentoring in advancing women's careers in construction. *Journal of Construction Engineering and Management, 144*(10), 04018103.

Ministry of Manpower Singapore. (2021). *Skills framework for built environment.*

Ntembe, I. C., & Oteng-Abayie, E. F. (2016). Assessing the challenges facing women in the construction industry in Malawi: A case of Blantyre City. *Journal of Construction in Developing Countries, 21*(1), 87–101.

O'Reilly, K. (2015). Gendering the skill-biased technological change explanation of wage inequality in the construction industry. *Industrial Relations Journal, 46*(4), 281–297.

Ojo, O., & Ajayi, A. E. (2020). Women in the construction industry: A case study of Nigeria. *Journal of Building Performance, 11*(1), 1–9.

Roscigno, V. J., & Hodson, R. (2004). Diversity, social capital, and cohesion. *Annual Review of Sociology, 30*(1), 459–478.

Royal Institute of British Architects. (2022). *Diversity and inclusion in architecture.*

Sen, A. (2001). The many faces of gender inequality. *New Republic*, 226(22), 35–39.

Shimizu Corporation. (2021). *Diversity & inclusion*.

Teo, M. M., & Loosemore, M. (2001). Gender and leadership style in construction. *Construction Management and Economics*, 19(1), 89–98.

UN Women. (2015). *Progress of the world's women 2015–2016: Transforming economies, realizing rights*. United Nations Development Fund for Women.

UN-Habitat. (2019). *Gender in the city: An overview of trends and challenges in Africa*. United Nations Human Settlements Programme.

UNESCO. (2021). *Changing the narrative: Girls' education in STEM in Asia and the Pacific*.

United Nations. (2021). *Empowering women in Kenya's construction sector*.

United Nations Economic Commission for Africa. (2018). *Women's entrepreneurship in Africa: Impacts of the world bank group's gender entrepreneurship and markets (GEM) program*.

Women in Construction Europe. (2022). *Breaking the mold: A look at women in construction*.

Women in Construction Europe (WICE). (2021). *Homepage*.

World Bank. (2019). *Women, business, and the law 2019: A decade of reform*. World Bank Group.

World Bank. (2022). *Women, business and the law 2022*.

World Health Organization. (2020). *Women's health in the European Region: A progress review*.

Yonhap News Agency. (2020). *South Korea pushing to break down gender bias in the construction industry*.

Yu, Y., Shen, L., & Leung, M. Y. (2017). Women's participation in the construction industry in China: Career progression and barriers. *Construction Innovation*, 17(1), 23–43.

Printed and bound by CPI Group (UK) Ltd, Croydon, CR0 4YY

13/06/2024

14515213-0002